Wisdom of Ramadahn

45 Thought
48 Negative thought
50 Harmony

This book has been compiled from the teachings of Ramadahn, a spirit guide speaking through his entranced medium Ursula Roberts. His tape recorded words have been transcribed by Muriel Hill and Audrey Ward in the hope they will give a measure of comfort, upliftment, or guidance at a moment when you are in need.

When reading it is sometimes necessary to remember that he frequently refers to human people as spirits, meaning spirits incarnate in human bodies. This may confuse readers accustomed to thinking of spirits only as discarnate entities.

Wisdom of Ramadahn

by

URSULA ROBERTS

Compiled by Audrey Ward

Regency Press (London & New York) Ltd
125 High Holborn, London WC1V 6QA

ISBN 0 7212 0846 0

Printed and bound in Great Britain by
Buckland Press Ltd., Dover, Kent.

Contents

CHAPTER ONE

Questions About Incarnation

Does a spirit choose a particular body and come to earth at a certain time so that conditions will be right to obtain the experience needed?

In theory this is so, but in fact when the spirit comes to take hold upon its bodies it will forget many of the theories and original purposes as it becomes enmeshed in the life of the earth. Our teaching is to help each one to regain the realisation of their identity as a spirit using the body for purposes of experience rather than being a body with a vague spirit form.

Must we always come in a body?

No, not all spirits incarnate. There are certain cleansings undertaken by some spirits who feel responsible for the errors of a past experience so some return in a body while others stand by and help. Spirits also enter the atmosphere of earth to work through a medium or to use one as a channel through whom blessing may be released, as with those dedicated to nursing, healing or surgery, or of work in which they try to lead a body of people unto greater truth. In doing these things each will find he has to contend with earth's ignorance, dissensions if he is a priest or teacher, selfishness and hatred if a leader of a nation. But each, as they fulfil their work, will have around them a group of spirits who are also engaged in trying to cleanse the earth of its weight of woe.

What if we find ourselves in a body we dislike?

There are many in this state—even as there are many who wish they did not live in the house they occupy—because the experience becomes hard and bitter and each one desires to escape the lesson. But it is wise to continue to the end with the realisation you are using the body only for a short season. Through this use you will bring the greatest degree of good to the earth.

What is the difference between soul and spirit?

Spirit is the subtle, indestructible, divine manifestation while the soul, which is composed of the fine mental and emotional bodies, is the being through which the spirit manifests.

Why do we lack awareness that we have a soul and a spirit?

As you enter your life experience the soul body and the physical body become closely interblended, especially when there is a good state of health and energy between the two. Therefore the best method to gain self-realisation is to withdraw your attention and say: "Which part of me is acting? Which part is thinking? What is it within me which says I do not know of my spirit?" It is not the mind, not the heart, nor yet the body; that in you which says who am I? That is it!

At what stage does the spirit enter the body? If it is pre-physical birth, what happens in the case of a still-born child?

The spirit may be near a woman, seeking life, for some while before the actual moment of conception. The joining to the actual growing foetus body comes about when there is a quickening or movement within the mother's womb, but the spirit may be conjoined and waiting within the area of the mother for some while before this happens.

When a child is born and the physical body is not able to retain life, the soul and spirit together have touched the vibration of the mortal world and have formed the nucleus of the soul bodies. These bodies will then continue to grow and develop within the regions of the spirit world. Here, spirits who have great love and wisdom tend and care for these infant souls. The soul body grows and develops under the stimulation of movement, sound, and in the exchange of love one to the other, even as a soul is nourished on the earthly plane by the exchange of love and companionship.

An expectant mother often looks radiant and is at the peak of her health. Could it be because she has this second spirit around her?

This is so. It is imparting spiritual energies to her to aid in the formation of this new soul body.

In the case of a miscarriage, why does it frequently occur around the fourth month?

Sometimes the incarnating spirit is not sufficiently strong to retain its hold in creativity upon the body which is developing. It may seek another opportunity for incarnation.

Is this why it is often the first pregnancy that miscarries?

This is true.

In that case, are abortions wrong before the period of quickening in that they are denying a soul entry?

Yes, there are many who have questioned this. What is termed abortion—the violent termination of the development of the infant body—brings about shock to the spirit who is hovering, trying to seek incarnation, but even more than shock; sorrow because of rejection. Surely it would be wiser to use means to prevent conception of a body which is not desired, and that men and women learned to control the passions of their sexual bodies. Surely, too, it would be better and wiser if infants were brought into your mortal world to be nurtured and loved instead of this harsh thrusting of them back into the life of the spirit.

You have said there are seven spirits in an affinity or group. Does this mean there are some spirits guiding from the spirit world others who are in an earthly incarnation?

Yes, regarding affinities in the soul group, sometimes one, two or three may enter into any earthly incarnation while the others watch or guide from the spirit realm. Some may remain away from earth in the high clear light of the purer spirit places, but always, because there is unity between them, there is a telepathic link which can be strengthened at any time. When there is only one in the earthly realm you will say, "Here is one who is always lonely, who seeks hither and thither without fulfilment or rest, because those who are in attunement are not to be found on earth."

But when that one opens the spiritual mind and comes into unity with the spirit forces, then indeed do they discover great joy and abundant comfort, for the others of the group will reveal themselves and the loneliness will be healed. In your world the idea is held that affinity only applies to man and woman, but I say there are seven in the soul group.

Following on that idea, are the experiences of the earthly one imparted to those still in the spirit realms? Do they learn from those experiences?

Truly, for even as a drop falls into a cup of water imparting its colour or flavour to the whole fluid, so the experiences of the one will bring understanding to the others. When the seven are again united within the pure places of spirit, then there is enrichment and understanding from the sharing of their mutual experiences.

Can two people on earth previously have been part of a twin soul in spirit?

Yes. Quite frequently one may choose to enter into the life incarnation simply to give comfort and love to the other if the other half of this twin soul has chosen to endure a life experience of extreme difficulty.

If it is possible to meet souls from an earlier incarnation, why have they not progressed onwards?

They may remain static because they are aware of the particular lonely or difficult incarnation being undertaken by the one entering the mortal life. In the spirit world there are no limitations of time, so what may seem a long time in earthly measure may be but a short time in the measure of spirit existence.

Often ties of love and kinship seem to bind us, preventing us from doing what we desire?

Such a binding surely teaches you how to love those surrounding you without becoming completely absorbed in the affairs of your family and friends. When you come to know that you yourself are a spirit using your body for a time in this relationship, then you learn to give some part of yourself while retaining a kinship and understanding with the higher forces of life.

When we incarnate, are we destined to have certain difficult experiences, regardless of how hard we try to live a pure life?

Surely, for you are born into an environment which often has been planned before you entered your earthly body. You choose the soil into which the roots of your experience will sink. This means a certain choice is made as to nation, place, family, and the climate of opinion in which you may find yourself when you enter the earthly life. So you may be born into a Jewish or Christian family or into the family of an agnostic, and each will give you a certain atmosphere of thought, a soil from which you may gain some earthly experience. Then, as you move through the pattern of your life, certain events occur which will test either your strength, understanding, or involve you in some greater comprehension of the world, some fuller unfoldment of your spiritual mind. Within this broad outline of events you have choice and freedom of will to do as you please.

What purpose is there for one forced to live in isolation and loneliness?

One of the most important lessons is first to learn how to be separate, then how to come into unity once more. The spirit in its pure state knows a wonderful sense of joy and unity in the spirit existence: soul flows unto soul, thought flows unto thought of others, and love is a wonderful unity. Yet to learn how to be alone is a necessary lesson. Some spirits take their plunge into the mortal life that in their separation and loneliness they may realise again their true spiritual identity as spirit, separate from the body but acting through it into the mortal realm. Yet upon that spirit plane they may learn to be in unity with the spirit group, the great creative power, but they may only come to appreciate the beauty of this unity and love when they have sojourned for a while in loneliness, in apartness, in the isolation of a mortal existence.

Until you have learned separateness you cannot know the value of contributing you own personal aspect of understanding unto the whole group, the whole unity of life, for each spirit gains an identity particular to itself, and through this it goes forth to enrich and re-create in other spheres and places by the knowledge it has gained.

What is one's own identity?

Your identity is the core which lies at the centre of your soul. Your mental and emotional bodies have absorbed radiations from the men and women who have surrounded you, and as you go into your inner search for self realisation, so you must discover how much of your outer personality is that imposed upon you by your parents, what part you absorbed from your teachers and from those you have loved. When you have understood this, you may find deep within there is another part of yourself, that which sought knowledge and reached out in the desire for love and understanding—that inner part—this is your real self. Spiritual development, the unfoldment of spiritual understanding, becomes in essence a search to discover you own real self.

What is the reason for incarnation?

There are many reasons, but for those to whom I speak it is threefold. First, to gain experience, experience which can only be gained in the world of matter itself. The Master Creator has set upon the great string of existence myriads of worlds and stars, innumerable states of life. The living soul cannot know these places simply by thinking about them.

The spirit learns by experience, by contact, and so gains knowledge of the creativeness which lies within himself.

The second reason is to learn to master earth's forces: the great forces of heat and cold, of attraction and repulsion, the powers of the air, the mighty winds which would blow you hither and thither. You master these forces that your existence may continue through the physical body, and as you do so, you also master the instrument through which the will of your spirit is expressed. You learn to control your hungers, the desires which draw you, and so inevitably you come at last to master the emotions, the feelings, angers and loves. If this were taught in your youth you would not allow yourself to be tossed this way and that by your appetites and anxieties, but instead you would know that the great challenge of life is to overcome.

When you realise mastery, then you can fulfil the third great reason for incarnation, the transmutation, or cleansing of the soul of the earthly world by imparting to it some quality of your own spirit which will cleanse, enrich and beautify it.

Sometimes your creative efforts may be in forming a body through which another spirit may come into the earth. Do not despise this action of the creativeness of life, but undertake it with reverence, understanding the privilege of creating a body through which a beautiful spirit may come into the ensoulment of the earthly world.

So, first you come to learn, secondly to master and thirdly to contribute something of love, a pattern of beauty, a restoration of harmony, a bringing forth of healing.

Teach your children the purpose of life, that they may no longer be sucked down into the whirlpools of negative thought and wrong impressions. Be sure that you give out light, love and forgiveness in all your thoughts, words and actions.

If we return to earth for another experience, are we affected by our previous aura?

Truly, but not all people using a physical body today have lived in the earthly world previously. There are many planets and worlds in which the soul may learn its lessons. Here within your earth there are many souls coming from less developed planes of experience, to be taught and to blend with people who have experienced it before. But there are some who have lived not once but many times with a mortal body, and they bring with them certain radiations, a spiritual aura which contains qualities gained in a previous time of living. Thus there are some who know instinctively how to live, to teach, to create music, to unfold earth's finer forces. Sometimes they know also in their inner consciousness what they wish to do and achieve in their present incarnation.

If we reincarnate, do we marry the same person again?

Possibly. Where there is extreme love in a previous experience and the man and woman were not able to remain together in harmony, and died with a great longing to live life on earth together, then they may enter again into earth's atmosphere for this purpose. But it is more usual for one who has had a previous life experience to meet or become partnered to a spirit of a differing experience because each come to learn a new lesson.

We talk so much of the many incarnations the spirit may undertake, yet it is your present incarnation that is fraught with a most important destiny. Try to withdraw your mind sometimes from consideration of what you were, or even of what you will be, into the thought that if you can live now to the highest and fullest of your ability then you are making the best use of the treasure of time which the great Master Creator has granted unto you.

Even the fleeting moments can be made golden with joy and fruitful with love. Do not destroy them by regret. When sorrow, frustration and hopelessness press in upon you, if you cannot bring joy into being, instil into the living moments the thought of peace, thus shall you make the best use of you present incarnation.

Is karma something to do with one's return to this planet?

Karma is simply a word which embodies the law of sowing and reaping. If you take an earth experience and sow no seeds of harmfulness, neither hurting nor destroying creation nor bringing harm to the soul of the world, then there may be no reason for you to return to outwork a karma. Your karma should be to sow in the times of your earthly life harmony, love, truthfulness and cleansing light, then you are sowing with good seed. When you leave your earthly body you will reap the result of such a sowing. Your karma may carry you forward into a further life of progress in the spirit regions.

Why do some people have distorted, imperfect bodies?

The spirit, in forming its being and entering the earthly life, comes into conflict with great currents of thoughts and tides of feeling that have been impressed upon the ethers by people who have incarnated before. Thus the spirit may find that the mind or body is strongly influenced by religious or racial prejudice in the community of that place. The sensitive spirit, feels this tide flowing against it, may not be able to combat it completely. You will see the effect as distortion in the vehicle which the spirit has made.

There are many forces and tides which affect each individual person. The one who knows that he or she is spirit will easily overcome these great tides of feeling and retain their own identity. But the one who feels that only the body and mind are important, will be swept into the great racial and religious currents of war and persecution.

Teach your brothers and sisters they are spirits using their bodies and minds, then they will be able to shift the emphasis of consciousness from the mortal to the immortal self. Thus shall you bring healing not only to the body and mind, but to these great streams of influence left upon the earth by past generations.

What about these poor unfortunate babies who are born without hands? Will they be compensated?

Although some are poor and unfortunate you must remember that life is a very large and wide circle of experience, and there is life before this earthly body as well as after. Sometimes men and women, who in a previous time of existence have ignored the usefulness of their hands or deprived others of the use of theirs, may choose to return to earth to learn how hard it is to be without such a tool, that in the wideness of experience they may truly value all the faculties which the Master Creator gives unto them.

Could such a disability be the result of resentment in a past life?

Not so much resentment as neglect. Often those who have been rulers or in positions of high power and who have ordered that their subjects for some small offence are deprived of the use of their hands, when they come into the spirit life may view what they have done differently. Then, with a deep sense of regret, on reincarnating they come minus the use of their hands.

There are others who on entering the mortal life may see a possibility of certain imperfections in the body, but think that they are strong enough to overcome them. Always the soul is compensated for its time of weakness: always it gains knowledge by such experience.

Why is there so much sorrow, suffering and pain in the world?

When you retain your awareness of spiritual reality, seeing that all this is but a passing thing, you can live through all the experiences of your world without too great a suffering or pain, for you will not allow yourself to become too deeply immersed in the changing activities of your world. You are souls and spirits of light and beauty, and have an identity which is wider and greater than this which you know at the moment. This mortal existence is but a flowing pattern, a passing thing, and the reality is the spirit, the soul. It is in what you learn from the world of matter that the importance of your incarnation comes.

What about old people who are bedridden and blind or deaf? It seems they are not learning anything. Why are they not freed by death?

If they had been wise, they would have sought to learn lessons of patience in the earlier seasons of their experience, but by the goodness of the Great Power, often a longer span is given unto some souls that they may learn lessons more completely and so bring their treasures into the spirit realm with them. So what appears to be a punishment, or an unjust or bitter experience, is in itself a blessing, but the blessing will not be revealed until the life journey is completed.

CHAPTER TWO

What Happens When We Die?

Ramadahn, can you say what you know about death?

Beloved brothers and sisters, we of the spirit have died our deaths. Because of this we are able to speak with understanding on this matter of life and death? Which each of you come to experience in your own short seasons of earthly existence.

The threads of life and death are woven together in a most wonderful and mystic pattern: it is as impossible for us to disentangle the threads, as it is for you, for they are each a part of the other. Where there is life, death is beginning to manifest. When death is taking place, there too is the dawning of life, for they are woven finely with a wondrous twinning of eternal life.

Would you tell us something about the reception at death?

There are many ways this may come into being. Often, as the body becomes aged and the soul gets ready to break forth into the new life of the spirit, a beautiful time of preparation begins.

On your earth, those acquainted with the one who bears life will begin their preparation by creating garments and conversing together as to the joy of the life still to come. Even so, here within the spirit realm, those who have known the soul soon to be released from the body will begin their preparation long before the ripening is completed.

Sometimes they will break through earth conditions to bring unto the expected beloved a reassurance and welcome in the form of a dream or vision. Here, a place is prepared, often a simple room in one of the temples, dressed with blossoms and flowers from the gardens of healing, and into which we bring objects dear and familiar to the beloved. The mother, father or other loving spirit will sit silently waiting beside this new-born soul until the deep state of rest ceases to hold the consciousness. As they awaken they behold the smiling faces of those they lost long ago, but who wait now to welcome them into the newness of spirit.

What of those who die of disease in hospitals?

Each hospital of your earthly plane is inhabited by a legion of shining spirits whose task is to watch over those who suffer, to bring peace unto those who are restless, and to guide as best they may the hands of those who minister.

When they see a soul breaking forth from the encasement of the body they send forth into the ethers a call for the servers, that the beloveds of this one may come swiftly, to carry the soul high away into the homes of rest within the spirit atmosphere close to the hospital place. Truly we know much of death—the death and reunion that brings joy—but you see only pain and sorrow. Those of you who have borne children will know that you approach the final time with a certain apprehension because you know not what to expect, but later this changes into expectation and joy.

Those who learn the laws of the spirit will know that when they come to the moment of dying they will feel apprehension and fear, but they will remember to transmute this into expectation and joy, into the remembrance to look for the light as the moment of death approaches, that they may emerge from the dissolution of the body into the joy and wonder of spirit.

As you wait by the bedsides of your beloveds, in the quietness of thought and even with a spoken word, say: "Go forth in peace. There is nothing to fear. Go forth to meet those who await you. Look for the *light!*"

Remember that in life you are in the midst of death, and in death you are in the midst of life. Most surely, each of you in the fullness of time will come to the closure of your mortal life, and the closure too of someone dear and beloved to your heart.

What happens to those who die through accident, war, or by the hand of other men and women?

When this happens, fear and confusion close in upon the consciousness and the spirit is held within the near-earth region. But if such a one has been made aware of the teaching that at death they must look for the *light* and for the guide in the region beyond earth, then as they realise they are dying, this recollection will slowly emerge and they will begin to look away from the place of terror, from the horror which held their awareness, and start to move up toward the region of peace.

Because so many today live only for the things of the body and the earth, many spirits are held close to the earth, hovering around their place of dying, seeking only to come back again into a familiar environment, frightened and lost. Let this teaching of looking to the *light* be made more widely known, and then even those who die tragically will find their way out of the places of sorrow into the regions of peace.

Always send forth your prayer for light when you hear of one who died at the hand of another, or of those whose bodies are destroyed through accident or war, saying: "Be at peace. Look for the light. Seek for one who will lead you out of fear into truth." Your thoughts sent forth in love and enlightenment will reach these souls. They come to them as the speaking of the priest comes into the consciousness of those who hear his voice as they are dying. But those who die without the priest, or the reassurance which should come through their religion can be reassured as they hear thoughts and prayers which go forth into the region surrounding your earth, thoughts that can lead them out of their darkness and confusion into light and harmony.

How long is the time of preparation for the withdrawal of the soul from the body?

Sometimes as long as two years, though three months is usual. But in your earth today there are such deep, slow disease forces at work and your doctors devise means of lengthening the period of life. Often death is expected by us before it is allowed to take place upon earth.

What happens when a large number of people die at one time because of an accident?

There is a certain pattern of experience for each soul, but not necessarily a predetermined length of time. The importance is in learning the lessons of experience rather than in the time taken, so there may be some who can grasp or develop a quality of the soul in a period of twenty years which may take another soul seventy years. Where there is sudden death through accident, this is not always planned as part of the spirit's experience, but it will often be foreseen by the spirits watching over that one. There will have been an intuitive recognition of the possibility of such a dying, because there is still some preparation given. Such things are foreseen by the Guardian ones, but though warnings are given and intuitive impressions imparted, the peoples of the earth are so intent upon their own desires that often they disregard what has been conveyed.

What happens to those who deny the existence of God and who think that when death comes that is the end?

There are many who come to the closure of their life in this state of understanding. There are many who destroy the body of flesh that has clothed their spirit (suicides) and they say they are dead, yet they still live, for the spirit lives even beyond the belief of the mind and soul. So the unbeliever looks this way and that saying: "I am dreaming for I know I died yet I still live. How then shall I destroy this which I know does not exist?"

This unbeliever must at last come to the acknowledged truth that he still exists, and looking round he will view life in the spirit regions, then looking back he will see the earth. As his vision circles again to spirit this one will see the beloveds, for truly every soul coming into this state is loved by somebody. There is the mother, father or grandparent, always somewhere there is a spirit in an affinity with this one, if not from the earthly existence then from the state before the mortal life began.

So the unbeliever is met with love, and these loving spirits will bring light into the shadows, truth to penetrate darkness, and slowly by creating opportunities for service, he will find his way upward into the regions of light.

But not all unbelievers or agnostics are like this, for some have become lovers of humankind and lavished themselves in love and service for the betterment of the rest, and this in a measure is the symbol of their worship unto the great Master Giver of all.

What happens to little children when they die?

These child souls do, indeed, have a very special place in the spirit world and a very special task to perform. This is not always understood by those on earth.

If death intervenes for the child, youth or maiden, as the physical body is laid upon one side the young soul is taken by the teachers and loving spirits into the regions of light and gardens of peace, that therein development and unfoldment may be completed in the care of wise and loving spirits.

Because it is the spiritual law that every soul grows through the giving of itself, so the child-soul has to learn how to give some part of its energy, its love, some part of itself, ere ever it may absorb new energies, truths and loves. So the children are trained and developed in the schools of the spirit and are then given some work to do, but these tasks are of the soul and the spirit.

What do the spirit children do?

Some come into earth's atmosphere from time to time to blend their influence with that of earth's dwellers, shedding and sharing the love inherent within the emotional body. As they shed it there, so do they become aware of the heaviness, weariness and loneliness experienced by those in the mortal world.

They come also to your little meditation and development groups, for as you sit thus, often a soul sinks into stagnation, and instead of peace there is heaviness and sleepiness. But when the children circle round such a group they impart a quickening vibration of power and joy: as the children dance and sing their vibration often emits a sparkling dust of radiant light which may be seen to the clairvoyant eye.

As they give of themselves in this fashion, so are they filled with new understanding, and on returning to the spirit school they will be full of questions: Why are the dwellers in the earthly life encloaked in grey? Why is the atmosphere so heavy? Why are my parents who love me so tearful? What is the purpose of earthly existence? As these children learn the truths and understand the lessons, they may in time be able to give to some growing medium a part of their knowledge and truth. By blending with a medium they bring to earth's people their simplicity,

purity and inward wisdom. At the same time they garner knowledge of
the difficulties and problems associated with life on earth.

In your great hospitals there are wise and lovely spirits, women who
in their earthly existence served as nursing nuns or sisters and who still
continue their ministry of love in these places of illness. These people
send forth requests unto the spirit children, who come and share their
joy with the hospital children who, in their bodies, are weary with pain
and sickness. The groups of spirit children will lift the soul of the sick
child to regions of light and healing that when the child wakens from
sleep it will be better able to deal with the unhappy state of the mortal
body.

Sometimes such children will be aware of their spirit companions,
but those in the mortal body will not always understand, and will think
that the child in its illness is becoming deranged in the mind.
Sometimes, too, the children will minister to the aged and lonely, who
are often very close to spirit, and the old ones waiting for the call to
spirit will be comforted. And the burden of loneliness will be lightened.

How do the children develop?

In the regions of spirit life the children also have their play, and we
often enter into their little games, teaching them some of the wisdom of
spirit. The joyous children run and fling themselves into our arms. As
we enfold them, we encircle them with the stronger spiritual force we
ourselves possess, as well as partaking of the child's joy.

They are also taught to circle round and to dance, and in their
rhythmic movements they absorb some of the ethereal matter inherent
in the spiritual atmosphere, instead of absorbing food. The ethereal
body is strengthened by this, the love body is quickened by the
exchange of love between itself and the loving souls who care for it, and
the mind is strengthened and quickend by question and answer, even as
on the earth.

But how beautiful are the children! Their eyes shine with the
unstained purity of the spirit, their bodies unfold in flexibility and
beauty, for any sickness left from the earthly experience is eradicated by
the healing and understanding of the spirit healers.

So, think sometimes of these children whom you love, not with
sorrow, but with joy and tenderness, and visualise them taking their

way through the schools of spirit, cared for by the mother and father souls, the servers and lovers of children, who in their love prepare them that in their turn they may bless and heal earth's loved ones.

What happens when children die as a result of war?

We gather up these young souls which have been shattered by explosions, for those suddenly thrust from the body also feel the effect of this in the etheric body. We bring them to great gardens and pools of peace, and special healers look after these child souls. After a long period of rest and correct teaching, in which they learn to absorb again the etheric atmosphere, the etheric body can be healed and restored, and the expansion of the love and mental bodies continued. We understand their needs, and if in some future time they desire to take again the earthly experience they will enter it without fear or shrinking, but with love and understanding.

What is the spirit view of euthanasia?

Our view of the difficult subject upon which you so often think is this: Let love be your watchword. Teach this unto those whom you meet day by day, and if love dictates their decisions then wise and beautiful will be their ways of solving the problems of human relationships.

We of the spirit know that life is an ever-flowing pattern, an ever-changing melody, a continuous process of living and being which is unbroken, for it is constantly transmuted from one shape into another. But you, encompassed around by limiting conditions, are not always able to see the eternities of time and the ever-changing pattern of creative life, so your understanding of life and death is somewhat different to ours. You regard death as an end; we see it as we regard birth, but an important incident in the whole flow of life. So, reach out and turn your vision past the ending of mortal life to the life beyond, then turn your vision back to the pre-birth existence, that you may see this is all part of the beauty and power of the Master Creator.

Whatever causes the termination of life on earth, whatever breaks the pattern, always there is understanding love, the great flowing life-force to reform it and bring harmony and beauty once more into being.

Therefore, when man or woman is helplessly suffering and others try to bring what may be a merciful end to their suffering, we see it but as a little break in the weaving pattern of human experience. Life continues, for life is a continuous pattern.

If upon your roadside you see a living animal which, through carelessness of its owner, has been allowed to stray and has become injured by a moving machine, beholding this creature panting and crying in pain, do you not see an act of ignorance which has broken the beautiful pattern of life? Do you not then consider which is the most loving thing to do: to heal the animal of its hurts, though even when its bones are mended it may only hop or move with pain to seek its food, or does your love for the creature bring you to release it from its suffering that its life may continue in this flowing pattern of the great Master Creator?

Love will dictate your decision. If your love is self-seeking you may hold it within its pattern of suffering that you can retain its companionship, but later you will be forced to think: "Was it real love that kept the living force within a body that is blind and crippled?"

So it is through all the pattern of human existence. As you sit beside the aged ones whom you love, whose bodily tenement has become filled with pain either because of the physician's ignorance or their own lack of attunement, sometimes the greater love is to release the spirit into the great flow of life within the spirit existence. But always the decision must be made in love, and sometimes it should be dictated by the desire of the sufferer himself.

First then, there should be the effort to restore harmony by bringing peace to the mind, spiritual healing to the body and soul, and love to the heart of the sufferers. If after that there is still pain, helplessness and disease, then sometimes the way of restoring harmony in life is to bring about release, for release is peace.

When a person dies, are they affected by the grief and sorrow of those remaining?

Excessive grief creates considerable disturbance in the consciousness of the one freed from the body, and within the heart aura of the one remaining grieving creates a funnel effect in which there is a continuous swirling movement. If the spirit loves the one who is grieving, then it becomes sucked into this funnel. Because of the magnetic attraction between the two the spirit will find it difficult to escape. People should be taught to send out thoughts of comfort and love to the departed one, and this will close the funnel and help to reassure the spirit as it goes forward to reunite with those waiting to welcome it.

Would you say it is wrong to grieve?

No, I think it is impossible for the human heart not to feel some sorrow when a dear one is freed from the physical body. But true love, understanding of spiritual laws, and knowledge that the spirit is freed from pain should bring gladness which will go with the departed one as a golden wave of joy.

Many people nowadays ruin their lives with drink, drugs, suicide or other abuse. How do they manage when they die?

If people on earth send out thoughts and loving prayers for them, this creates a candle flame of hope which lightens the greyness into which they cross, a greyness formed by their own hopelessness and lack of effort. Then when the serving spirits see these golden flames of prayer they discover the ones in greyness and will lavish love and understanding upon them, perhaps drawing towards them some spirit belonging to the family circle, maybe a grandparent who has known them in infancy, for the love of grandparents and parents for spirits such as this is very deep and compassionate. As this love flows around them they are warmed, some of the greyness is dissolved, and in time they are taught to serve, to give something of themselves, and then indeed they begin a gradual progression.

Where death takes place and the body is left for medical research, would this in any way hinder the spirit's evolvement?

It may hinder the evolvement if the spirit to whom the body belonged did not bequeath the body for this use. But if the departing one freely left the body for this purpose, then in the after-death state that spirit will remember this, and may sometimes come to look with interest at the discoveries being made with the discarded body. But if that body was seized and used without the wish of that spirit, then indeed it will be distressed, and may often be held to the body because it does not wish the research to take place.

At a burial, parsons pray and sanctify the body before it is buried. Does this have any effect on the spirit?

This will depend upon the power of the priest, for not all are true priests in the meaning that they are able to channel high spiritual force. Some simply repeat words in a book, or go through motions they have been taught. A true priest, understanding the power of spiritual force, may create around the burying place a protective envelope of spiritual power which will protect the body and soul from harmful forces, and may also aid the spirit to move into higher regions of understanding.

What happens to those who commit suicide?

There is no mighty spirit who metes out judgement to those who end their earthly life, no god within the distant heavens who banishes them unto the regions of darkness, for here there are natural laws which govern the way of life even as there are upon earth.

You have compassionate men and women who seek out and minister unto those trying to commit suicide, and here also there are spirits filled with love and compassion who try to bring those who have ended their life in distress, out of this state into love and harmony once more.

But what happens to them will depend on the conditions under which the suicide occurred. If there was an indulgence in cruelty, and the suicide was an attempt to escape the judgement of others, then the wish to escape will still be strong in the after-death state, and such a spirit will continue to run away from others he may meet. If the departed one was not strong enough to deal with their earthly responsibilities, then their after-death state will be one of confusion, for they find they are not dead but still living. If one soul loved another so greatly and felt they could not continue without that companionship, then after death the loved one who previously died will invariably remain close, trying to lead that soul into better conditions of understanding.

But there are others, spirits of men and women who have terminated their life because they could no longer bear the agony of the body when it was being destroyed by disease. They say to us: "Spirits of Light! What terrible thing have I done? May I be forgiven?"

We hold their hands and turn their eyes upwards to the light, for these have already passed through the purifying processes of the body as disease destroyed the body itself. So we are able to lift them above the recollection of their pain into the clear and beautiful light of healing.

Some there are who, under the persecution of tyrants, have found that their future holds no hope, and in their isolation sometimes they too will terminate earthly existence. When we find them wandering within the grey spheres, seeing our light they turn to it saying: "Still the world is dark! Is there no hope, no joy anywhere in the universe?"

But we link them unto spirits who have loved them, that hope may be restored, and through this chain of light and love they may slowly be lifted into the light. The energy forces still present will gradually be dissipated through their serving and helping in the near-earth region or in the earthly world itself, and the persecuted suicide will begin to rise into higher regions of spirit life.

There are many reasons why earth's people come to the termination of their mortal experiences, and we wish that you would not send out to them thoughts of despair and horror, but rather lift them on prayers of light and thoughts of encouragement.

You speak of the grey spheres, and the near-earth regions. Why are those who die unnaturally held close to the earth?

When your spirit first entered the mortal world it formed bodies of feeling and thought as well as creating the etheric and physical bodies. All these become the person who is sitting quietly within this room, thinking: "I am I, I am myself." You are yourself, but you are greater than you know. Therefore, when your spirit relinquishes its hold upon your mortal and etheric bodies and eventually the body of feeling and thought, this withdrawal must be a gradual process, that the elements of the physical body may return to the earth, the power of the etheric may go back again into the aura of your world, and your spirit may continue for a while to learn its lessons through the bodies of feeling and thought—the soul—the vehicle of the spirit, when your earthly existence ceases.

If that existence is suddenly terminated, the bond between your spirit and mortal body may be broken, but the heavy emanations of the etheric body are not immediately exhausted, and this holds the soul and spirit unto the aura of your mortal world.

The physical body could be likened to the substance of water, the etheric to a heavy gas, and the soul body unto a lighter form of gas. Therefore, in the process of normal dying, the heaviness of the physical and etheric bodies gradually dissolve, so when the soul is freed it is able to rise as quickly and easily as a light gas. If there is sudden or unexpected death or suicide, then the soul is held down for a time by the weight of the energies in the heavier bodies, and until this is lightened or dissolved the soul cannot rise into the high regions of spirit life.

If someone who committed suicide was strongly influenced by another's thoughts, are they linked to that person in some way afterwards?

Yes, for they have absorbed certain radiations from the aura and they will hear the thoughts of that person as they are in the new after-death state. But there are bands of ministering helpers, those we call the missionary spirits, who are forever at work in the near-earth region and in the grey spheres, trying to aid spirits of this kind.

There is always hope and love, and there are always those who try to reach them, but when they are enwrapped in the shadow of their own despair it is not easy for us to find them, so an intermediary—often a person such as yourself—becomes of immense importance.

It cannot be easy to commit suicide; it must need a lot of courage. How do you feel about the word courage in this connection?

There are two aspects in all things, light and dark, weakness and strength, so there is also the opposite of courage which is sometimes called escapism. Many who terminate their life are at that time experiencing this opposite aspect of courage. But those who end their life prayerfully with deliberate intent, these have spiritual courage, and this becomes their virtue in the spirit life.

We are taught that no one is given more than he can bear, but this would not seem to be the case if people take their own life. They must come to a point where they just cannot bear any more?

This is only partly true, because all experiences should be aided by the love and care of family and community. If a soul in the earthly life is bearing or enduring a difficult burden, and if that one is forsaken by the companions who should strengthen and encourage them, then indeed the burden becomes too heavy.

In your world today, unity is becoming weakened, people are beginning to live in isolation instead of as part of a community or family. They often try to establish unity in a different level and fashion, isolating themselves from the family because they do not agree with their traditions and ideas, then becoming enfolded in new groups, organisations, circles, and when that happens, then the soul is again strengthened. But between arriving at the new unity and breaking with the old, they feel lost, alone and weakened. Each one who feels they cannot bear the burden any longer, or that their karma is too difficult, each one is really saying to the whole community: "You have failed to support me! You have failed to help or heal me!"

Sometimes suicides don't really mean to kill themselves. Is this a cry for help?

Truly, therefore the responsibility or the karma of the suicide is really upon the whole town, the whole nation, the whole family.

What happens to somebody like Adolf Hitler who is said to have committed suicide?

Such a soul descends into the place of shadows, and though for a while he may be comforted and helped by the spirits who love him, he has to be made aware of the repercussions of all that he created amongst his people, including the thoughts of all those whom he harmed and grieved. This will continue to vibrate around him until such time as he works his way out of that condition. But because at one time he desired the good of the community and had love for his mother and family, so there will be some love to soften and warm him in the midst of his confusion.

If there are spirits who see a potential suicidal type on earth, is not help given when that person is in the sleep state?

If we can reach such a one by means of symbolic dreams or teach them when they are sleeping we endeavour to do so, but each soul is living an experience special to itself, so it is not possible to say we do this for all souls.

If you help them in their sleep state, does that mean they do not actually come out of their body then?

Not all come into the spirit when they are sleeping; only those who are enlightened. Those who are engrossed with their body or immersed in self-pity seldom emerge in the sleeping time.

When people terminate their life, do they have to reincarnate to live through the experiences that led to the termination?

Some may wish to take another life experience if they feel they did not gain or learn all they desired. But there are infinite opportunities for advancement in the spirit spheres, and if such a soul wishes to give service to others and to develop the inner talents of his soul, he will be given that opportunity.

Many people in your present time feel hopeless, and when they find their way difficult, often they remember the peace of death which they have known in a previous time of natural dying, and as they remember, so suddenly there will come to them the desire to go back again into that peace.

It is for you to send them understanding, saying in your thoughts: "We know of your need, we give you our love. Look to the light, and rise up out of your distress."

Thus may you aid them upon their way, and also help the servers of spirit to lift them into the true light of spirit where they may again find opportunities for service, for this is the law and the way of the spirit.

What is the spirit view of cremation?

Cremation of the body is a good thing, but to understand this you must first know that each spirit is expressing through the body its own magnetic force, its own spiritual power. It leaves an imprint of this power upon everything it uses, the clothes worn, the tools used, all things touched day by day, and through this imprint myriads of tiny threads of magnetic force are established between itself and its surroundings. By this, each of you become part of your familiar environment, and the home, be it humble or great, provides a place of security and peace. When you become separated from these things, especially in old age or illness, the individual is weakened and seems to lose strength. If you are a person who loves your body and possessions then an ensoulment is created, this may hold the soul when you no longer use your body on departing into the state beyond death.

This law and teaching was understood in Egypt by the priests who knew that to retain the spirit influence of the kings, queens, rulers or wise men they could keep the body in such a state that the spirit could not easily pass beyond the region of its ensoulment with the body. So they embalmed the body, placing it in a familiar part of the land, surrounded with things beloved to that person, things imprinted with their own particular stamp of the soul and spirit.

Similarly is the entombment of the body in your Christian religion, for the body is placed within an encasement of lead and wood before burial, and the magnetic forces are only very slowly exhausted. I would say that such a practice is not good, for the spirit is unable to progress into the heights of spiritual experience or take another earthly life, if so it is needed, while the magnetic force is still retained within the mortal body it once used.

So it is good and right that people of earth have taken up the traditions of other races. There are those who follow the old truths of

India, and there are also those whom you call the Romany gypsies, who in their wisdom submit to the flames not only the body of the departed spirit but also the caravan in which he or she travelled. These Romanies understood the attachment of the soul unto its possessions by the magnetic forces of the soul body.

Is there a minimum time advisable before cremation?

Comfort the spirit ere ever the body is laid to rest. The spirit may hover near it for a time, therefore a period of three or four days and nights should be allowed before the body is brought to the purification by fire, for sometimes these who are your beloveds pass into spirit in a state of dreaming, sleeping their way out of the body consciousness under the influence of earth's medical drugs and medicines, and may hover in this half dream state near the body. Only when they hear the thoughts and prayers of those praying for them in their departure into the after-death state do they realise that death has intervened. Then the spirit, still in its dreamy half-drugged condition, will look around and see those who have come to welcome and lead it away into places of peace and joy.

How can we best help our spirit to leave the body at death?

If you are aware that your body is dissolving or that the life essences are leaving it, then by the use of your will and your breathing, you may assist this. Think firstly that you are slowly withdrawing energy from your feet, bringing it up through your legs by your will and your thought, upward to the region of your heart and lungs. Then transfer your attention to the brain and by a gentle out-breathing and use of your will bring your energies into the higher regions of the brain, the higher consciousness, by which time your soul energies will have gathered themselves together and you will be floating free of your physical body. Then those guardians who are waiting, will aid the severence of the cords which bind the mortal and soul bodies together, and will simply take you away to the spirit regions.

But to do this necessitates much thought in the years of your maturity, that as the body ages this remembrance will be firmly set within the spiritual consciousness. The use of this recollection will free you from fear of injury or death. You should also recall in your inner soul those who are your dearest and best beloveds, that coming forward they will accompany your new-born soul away from the body into peace.

What happens to a mother who dies still dearly loving a son upon earth who does not reciprocate that love?

When the mother passes to spirit, because of her love she will remain in the awareness of the son, and when he comes to lay upon one side his mortal body she will be there to greet him, for love creates an enduring relationship. But if he still continues to reject this love, then the harmonious relationship is dissolved and he will gravitate towards those more in attunement with his soul, while the mother will be drawn to a region wherein she can express her lovingness towards other souls or spirits with whom she is in harmony.

But this does not mean the total relationship will be dissolved, for she will still be able to see her son while her love continues.

What will happen to us when we leave this mortal world?

Your life will be firstly one of joyous reunion, then joyful surprise, then joyful fulfilment. In addition, when you have become accustomed to your life of the spirit, you may be taken to a place similar to your cinema in which you will see a reviewment of all your past life upon earth. As you sit there in quietude, your friends will leave you so that you may see all the details of your mortal life, your good and bad deeds, why you undertook some labours and neglected others. You will also see the manner in which your thoughts and deeds reacted into the lives of others who were linked to you by friendship, kinship, or work in the community. As you behold this reviewing of your life so you will see it as yourself. Some part of it you will regret, but no-one will judge you except your own self, for you will behold the manner in which you used your spiritual opportunities or neglected your chance to create good and harmony. When the seeing is complete you will either hide your face in your hands, creeping away into the shadows of the hall because you are afraid to look upon those who love you, or else you will lift up your eyes in gladness and see your friends with joy, because there were only a few things of which you needed to feel shame.

So, try to order your life now so that you will have nothing to regret when you come into the pure light of Spirit. This reviewment will be one of your difficult experiences, but because you will be surrounded by the love of understanding spirits you may be aided even in this time by their sympathy. If they hear you crying with an anguish of regret, loving ones may draw near to comfort and to show you how you may right the wrong by rendering service.

CHAPTER THREE

Life in the Spirit World

Can you tell us something of the spiritual plane you call the Summerland?

In this beautiful place, sometimes called the Summerland, sometimes Heavenland or the Life Elysian, all is harmony and beautiful colour.

When in your earthly experience you are conscious of calmness, and have an awareness of great beauty surrounding you in which you feel your unity with the great Giver of all Life, this is a dim reflection of the state which you will one day know when you pass from the confines of your mortal body into the freedom and light of the Summerland.

Here, there is no winter or summer, but there is a season in which life-waves of varying activity come to their fullness and die silently away. It is as if for a season a golden life-wave brings a golden radiance to all things, and as this dies away it is replaced by a green lifewave, and for a while there is a greenness within all. The variety of colours known upon earth all come into manifestation in turn, bringing into bloom blossoms which belong to their particular strata, so the colour waves touch everything, transforming, changing and beautifying.

The best way to understand this is to visualise yourself standing in some great peaceful valley with gentle waters flowing through. From time to time there is a mighty rainbow, or lamp with rainbow colours, which slowly turns in its orbit, flooding the valley, touching the grassy hillsides and transforming the calmness of the water with the differing shades reflected.

Because there is no season of cold or heat we do not need dwelling places which are enclosed or roofed, so structures are erected for our use similar to the ancient temples, with raised pillars through which curtains can be hung or foliage trained to create privacy, for the habit and need to withdraw is still felt. These temples are sometimes left open, that the light from a higher realm may stream through, bringing a concentrated blessing unto those who commune within.

Here too are temples wherein spirits may gather into congregations, and upon altars are set, not symbols of religion as you know them, but vessels of transparent light, mirrors which capture and reflect the concentrated light as it falls from higher planes. Through these pure mirrored surfaces light may shine to bless and illumine those who come to commune, worship, and to uplift their thoughts, desiring that even from this beautiful plane they may rise higher to gain experience in other realms of beauty, drawing forever nearer to the great Pure Light which is beyond the comprehension of man in his present state, but nevertheless seen by him in the spiritual vision when dwelling in the Summerland.

Do spirits grow older there, as people age in earthly life?

Within this realm there is no ageing, and in reality, no youth. There is the shining soul maturity of those who come carrying the burden of experiences garnered from many years of earthly understanding, but the body they use is free from age and stands in the beauty of its maturity. Those who grow from infancy or youth within the spirit realm, these too mature slowly to adult form, but they retain within the inner spirit the radiant purity of their joyful childhood.

Even as I try to lay before you the vision of this beautiful place, would it not be good to so order your lives that when you come to the ending of your earthly journey you pass swiftly into this place? So, day by day, think not that what happens to you is of importance and grieve not over the actions which others extend to you, but rather think unto yourself: 'The wisdom of the spirit lies not in what others do, but in how I react unto what others may do.'

Order your life so that your reaction is always one of forgiveness, gentleness, peacefulness, lovingness. So will your spirit become lightened and brightened, and at the end of the journey it will be released, ready to rise into the realm of light where it may enjoy all the happiness, harmony and beauty which I strive so inadequately to clothe in the words of earth, that you may gain some faint understanding of the beauty you may all see one day.

Can you give us a description of that part of the Summerland in which you live?

I would describe it in this way. There is a temple situated at the foot of a mountain, and running through the centre of this temple is a stream of pure water. Upon the sides of this flowing stream are mossy banks and little grottos in which Indian spirits may come to rest, to meditate and to draw fresh power ere some new ministry is undertaken on the earth. It is from this stream of healing or purification that the spirit known as Rushing River draws the influence he endeavours to impart through his medium, for the stream can be diverted, or used by any individual who so desires.

Also within this temple are kept scrolls which relate to the further work we plan to do, and special scrolls or books to which I myself may refer when giving a specific teaching on a subject unfamiliar to me but good for those on earth. This corresponds to a library, and is my place of study and meditation.

Within this temple is the hall of rest wherein many spirits still joined to their earthly bodies can come during sleep or entrancement, to absorb the atmosphere of peace and inspiration which may help them in their further progression. At the far end of this temple is a gateway of silver filigree. We only open these gates at special times of festivals or recreation, and when we do, it reveals a shining pathway by which we may go upward upon the mountainside to attend festivals of reunion. There we commune with those of a more advanced nature who give us a baptism of power, that upon our return we may bring fresh power to cleanse and harmonise the conditions wherein we work near the earthly plane itself.

Around this temple is a rolling grassland with trees; children come and go, and the souls of the weary sometimes come to rest here. It is not a permanent structure, but one we have raised for our special work, and when our time of service unto earth is completed, the temple will dissolve silently away.

What about those who died defending their country? What do they do in the spirit life?

Some of those who fought and swept the world with fire, after their transfer into the spirit existence, say unto the spirits of wisdom: "For what purpose was all the effort? I did not desire to create harm, but that was all I could do. Can I now do something for the creation of peace?"

So here in the spirit places a great army of peace has been formed, soldiers, sailors and airmen of the past whose simple desire is to establish peace. They now belong to the great armies of peace in the spirit world, and when there is a threat of war on earth, or when it seems the ways of men are bringing a great crisis into being, the clairvoyants on earth may say they see the coming of the armies of light into the atmosphere of the world. They come not to fight with the weapons of destruction, not with destructive fire, but with their purified will which has become like a gleaming sword. They fight with their thought, which goes forth with vibrations of peace into your mortal existence.

How do spirits communicate with each other?

The language of the spirit is the language of thought, and we who dwell within the spirit existence learn to use thought more and more directly. I can only speak from my own understanding and experience.

In the plane where I dwell I may desire to convey to another spirit the knowledge that one still in the earth life needs strength and light. So, I think of that person, clothing the thought in the shape of a circle to show the other spirit that I am thinking of one encircled by the hard shell of earthly experience; then often I complete the message by picturing a shining golden star. Thus they will understand that an earthly one is troubled and needs the gold of spiritual hope. So that spirit may go swiftly unto the earth to impart to that mind a star-like golden thought to give encouragement, light and strength, and in the fullness of time in it will be said, "Truly spirit heard my prayer and brought unto me the light I needed."

Within the first plane of spirit we have schools where those newly come are taught how to use their power of thought. Often you ask about them, saying: "What are they doing?" How can we explain in the simple words of earth that these men and women, whom you considered wise in their earthly years, are at school learning how to think! Not many of you learn to use your power of thought correctly or constructively. You allow your thoughts to go this way and that, wasting energy in thinking thoughts which create hopelessness and destruction in the future rather than peace and harmony.

Consider how it will be when you yourself have died and are living again in the spirit existence. You may come close to the earth, wishing to convey comfort unto your mother, brother or to the child whom you love, but they do not hear your thought nor know you are near. Therefore you as spirit must wait patiently until such time as they are in a state when the mind is at rest, or when they turn from their grieving to the remembrance of you. Then, standing by, you create by thought a memory picture of your appearance, or of a place, or something your loved one will remember as being associated with yourself.

You will have to concentrate all your effort on thinking what will comfort that one, then silently gathering together all your will power, project it on to the mind of that one you desire to help. But because you are anxious and unaccustomed to this communicating, your thought picture may be distorted and the earthly one will shake his head and say, "What strange thing is this which comes before my mind?"

To such spirits we say: "Do not try to create a complex thought picture, but visualise a light, a colour or blossom which the loved one on earth, seeing and beholding, may know comes to them from spirit."

Your thoughts from the earth unto spirit need to be trained. From your minds should begin to vibrate thoughts of gentle love, of rose-pink encouragement and tenderness unto those spirits who wish to return to you. Thus as you learn to think thoughts of creative beauty now, so are you training yourselves to think well and beautifully when you come to the closure of your earthly life and continue in the planes of the spirit existence.

On earth you marvel that you are able to prove the reality of telepathic power. What childlike thing, what foolishness is this, that the spirits of men and women using the mortal brain and body know so little about the language of the spirit that they know not that it is one of thought? It should be natural for you to exchange thoughts with each other, to project thoughts of gentleness, healing and understanding, for this is but the speaking of spirit unto spirit, just as it will be when you come to the closure of your earthly life.

What do we need to do in order to progress quickly in the spirit world?

What may cause you to stand waiting for a long time at certain gates of understanding lies hidden deeply in your own consciousness. So, try to consider what it is within yourself that holds you back from wider progression. Let go of regret and let go of self reproach. Say sometimes in your prayer: "Yes, great Father of All, I have failed in this. I should have done better. Help me next time to fulfil this with a greater understanding."

Do not weep over your failure and reproach yourself endlessly, for you only build a barrier which holds you back from Light and comfort. Self-pity cannot help you. Others may pity you, but pitying yourself enfolds you in garments which will clog and hinder your progression. Rather, think unto yourself: "Yes, I have walked this difficult way, searching in loneliness for my treasures in darkness, but others too have walked this way and have been glad. I too will be glad!"

The gross errors of fear, selfishness, hatred and jealousy are like old garments, which belong not to brothers and sisters such as yourselves. But beware the garments of regret and self pity, and also beware the robes of superiority. Be not like some who, having gained understanding and the power to serve, feel that they are superior to their brothers and sisters, for their very state of superiority creates around them an armour which may, until it has been laid on one side, prevent them from going forward in the garments of humility which will clad them in the great Summerlands of joy.

They may take you and teach you how to return to the atmosphere of your earthly world. How can Spirits help a guilty soul feel less guilty? That by silently standing by you may shield a child whom you neglected in your time of earthly existence. The child may not be aware of your influence, but as you stand there giving strength and protection, so some part of this neglect will be alleviated. A great part of the serving of the spirit to your mortal world occurs in this way. Spirits come back to shield, guide and strengthen or to give goodness into the world, because they are conscious of the disharmony they created during some of their seasons of mortal existence. So even if you have sinned or done harm do not torment yourself feeling that all is lost, rather remember you may clear this by doing greater good, by comforting the sick and lonely, and by sowing wisdom and peace in the later years of your mortal life.

If we are all in different states of evolvement, does this mean that everybody goes through the same after-death process of rest and cleansing?

No, for according to your degree of evolvement will be your consciousness when you come into the spirit existence. It may be possible for you to pass through the state of dying with a full awareness of what is taking place, and therefore you may come with a feeling of joy and will not need sleep, nor yet cleansing. But most certainly you will experience joyful reunion ere ever you pass on to the next state of working, serving or expressing, according to your state of understanding.

Having died, some souls do not realise they are dead. Why is this? Have they not a spirit guide or guardian who can tell them?

Some people come to the end of the mortal life with such a fixed idea in their mind that they will not accept there is a condition of life beyond death; they are unable to realise they are still living although the mortal body has died. It is impossible to penetrate through an area of fixed created ideas because this forms something similar to a shell around that spirit. Although there may be those who will show them and explain this, if they reject the explanation then there must be a waiting time until they are willing to accept it, even as in the mortal life you may explain something to your brother or sister and even reiterate it, but if they are determined not to listen to you then your explanation will be useless.

If one of a family progresses more than another on earth, will the whole family be together in spirit?

They will be together for a brief while, for the great law of love governs the way of the spirit state. So whether you are high or low in your progression, still the law of love, unity and joy will manifest itself. Even those who have known great spiritual progress in the earthly life are not divorced from simplicity, for this is part of their growth and will bring them into the simple joy of the family group, that the simplicity may be expressed in the wholeness of the pattern.

Is the music that one hears in the world of spirit something entirely celestial and beyond our comprehension, or is it similar to our own music?

This will depend upon which region of spirit you may be entering. If you are in the first region surrounding the mortal world then the music will be very similar to that to which you are accustomed, but if you are able to move into the region where the musicians are active or even into the spirit gardens where the blossoms are sounding forth their own true note, then you will be aware of a differing music which you may find difficult to translate into the familiar sounds you know in the mortal life.

Are there people from other planets in the spirit world?

Truly, there are some who come and visit from other planets from time to time, just as there are some from high regions of spirit who may visit other celestial bodies. But when a spirit has moved out of the radiation which surrounds your immediate earthly planet it is not always easy for them to return, but certainly under some conditions there is movement to and fro.

In the spirit world do we still have the same emotions and feelings as on earth?

Your emotions will relate very much to the particular force under which you are operating. In the first stage, in the near-earth world, you may still feel the same greed, hunger, anger or desire for revenge. Such emotions hold the spirit very close to the earth where it may remain for a long time. But those who lived a normal life of reasonable emotion and loving kindness when upon earth pass swiftly into the first planes of the Summerland where harmony and love predominate, and certainly love will be the characteristic emotion of such a life. But there are others whose dominant key in their experience is in the mind, who are more developed in the body of thought and ideas, and these may pass quickly from the region of love into this other region where they seek knowledge, and in that one the emotion of love is not so dominant.

What is the total population of the spirit world?

This is something I cannot explain, because all entities form into groups which are sometimes like globes or circles, one, two, three or more blended together, and most labours are undertaken in these harmonious groups. As the whole atmosphere of the world of spirit is an expanding flowing freedom very similar to that of your sky, it is not possible to count spirits as you may count individuals in your mortal world.

I believe in the spirit world there is not time. Why can't you follow our time?

We can follow your time if we have communication with spirits who are still serving very closely with mediums or persons such as yourselves in the mortal atmosphere, for they will learn how to read your time vibrations. You have on your earth a clock which periodically gives forth sounds like a bell, and some spirits standing close by can measure time by that sounding bell. Then, too, earthly time is measured by your festivals, for when we see the myriad thoughts coming from earth's children in glory of preparation we know it is your Christmas season, and when we see you making prayers and joying in the blossoms we know it is Eastertime, and when we see emanating from you joyous thoughts when people have remembered you, we know it is the time of anniversary. But in spirit life we have no need for times of remembering, nor of the passing seasons, so we are happy to live in our timeless world, but if necessary we can become attuned to your earthly time.

You spoke once of the law of harmonious relationships; what does this mean?

The law of harmonious relationships is to be found in the twisting of the ropes bonded by thought and by love. As each soul moves forward into higher regions of spirit no-one can go alone, for always they draw another after them or take another with them, for this is surely the law of life.

Even so is it for you upon earth. As you move forward in your development and as your unfoldment of the soul continues, because of the twisting of the chains and threads of relationships, inevitably you lift somebody else one step higher as you move forward, and they in their turn bring another with them. And so this law of harmonious relationships, this linking together of all in joy and peace, means the slow but steady forward movement of souls through experience, higher and higher into every increasing regions of light, love and harmony.

CHAPTER FOUR

The Power of Thought

We hear a lot about the power of thought. Can you explain this from a spirit point of view?

Whilst you are in the mortal existence you seldom use your power of thought to construct anything in creative beauty. You are taught to absorb ideas and to remember teachings which relate to your mortal life, but you should learn during your childhood and youth how to create by the very action of your thinking.

Your children should be given trays on which are spread fine particles of delicate sand and little films of dust. They should be taught how their powers of thought can emit such a radiation from the cells of the brain and eyes that as they concentrate they can influence matter itself, until the particles begin to form themselves into beautiful crystaline patterns.

It should be possible for you to look upon a little living flame, and by the power of your concentration, either bend the flame or pierce the fine warm air surrounding it so the flame flickers and responds to the action of your thoughts. But you never even try these experiments to prove your mastery over earth's finer forces. You allow your thought power to be wasted in turning round and round in your mind with some little problem, or you fall into negative ways of thought by creating patterns which are inharmonious and sometimes harmful to yourselves and others.

This human body through which your will is expressed may be divided into three states, three levels. The level above your brow is filled with an intensity of ethereal matter that is light and spiritual and most easily affected by your constructive and holy thought. The level below the brow and into the region of the heart is where the etheric matter has a heavier vibration, and when thought is concentrated here it creates patterns and pictures of a differing degree. Below your heart and downward to your feet there is a heavier density of matter into which, quite often, your thoughts will pass, but they will relate very much to your physical body and the deeper thoughts of your heart.

The thoughts of most people are below the heart and are often inharmonious, turning round in a burrowing restlessness that can be likened to a little crab turning until it buries itself in the coolness of damp sand. As an inharmonious thought goes deeper into the cell matter of your physical body, burrowing like this crab, it penetrates, until it can be seen reflected on your body. It will show, either as disease, in a blockage within the circulatory system, or in falls that may injure the legs or feet. In injuring the lower part of your body you are reflecting an inward thinking that has preceded this over a long time.

The action of your thoughts takes longer to reflect into the denser matter of the lower person than does the higher spiritual thought from the region of the brain. So let your thought go out in harmony and strength to rebuild, reharmonise and heal that which you have made imperfect.

In the region below the brow are the organs associated with hearing, speaking, breathing and moving: all these sensitive organs are responsive to your thoughts. Do you ever think of listening to the music of the spheres, the sighing of the leaves, or the music created by the singing insects? Do you listen with sympathy to the crying of your brothers and sisters, or do you influence your delicate organs of hearing with your desire to be deaf to the cry of the unlovely and unlovable in your world? Do you give forth love or do you close your heart in irritability because the ones near you are demanding affection?

You are influencing your own organs by the very action of your thoughts. Think constructively, and reconstruct your own body out of patterns of illness and disease into harmony, beauty and health.

Learn to think from above the brow. Think the thoughts of the spirit self; direct the activity of thoughts of the heart and those below the heart, that all may be reconstructed into harmony and health.

There seems so little time. There is so much I want to do.

Time does not exist, except in your earthly consciousness. When you begin to raise yourselves away from your concern with the immediate small things of the earth and come into contact with things of the Spirit, you will find that a long time may seem but a moment, and sometimes a moment of your earth may be so filled with heavenly bliss that it seems an eternity of happiness. Therefore, free yourself and do not allow time to press upon you like the grey rain clouds which can cover your pleasant English land.

A small work faithfully accomplished is of great value in the fullness of time, but a long labour done with but heedless intent has no great value. There is all eternity before you, and the things you are learning in these years of your earthly life, the seeds you are sowing into the world about you, the creations of your thought, these will continue long after your body has ceased to weigh upon your soul. What you are creating now will be useful to you in the eternities to come, so free yourselves from the oppression of time, come into consideration of the things of eternity, and you will discover unrolling visions of beauty, vast spaces of light, and within yourselves will unfold powers which are the true spiritual enduring qualities of your soul and spirit.

Are you, Ramadahn, a separate identity, or are you a strata of thought which is congenial to the medium?

I would think I am a "strata of thought", for truly I spend much time in the realms of thought. If you possessed sufficient clairvoyant vision you would see me now as a shimmering vibration of colour or movement which we call the vibration of thought. I have an identity separate from the medium for I live my own life, think my own thoughts, and quite often visit my own friends—without the knowledge of the medium. Sometimes, too, I endeavour to answer questions coming from minds such as yours, and they will say I answered their question without their speaking to the medium.

If one is trying to help a person on earth who has close relatives or friends in spirit, is it helpful to send your thoughts to these spirits to ask them to help their beloved one?

Yes. Your thought, going to the one who is now free of the body, will often inform them of the condition and cause of the worry or illness affecting the beloved on earth. Often they will be aware that there is a cloud of anxiety or confusion, but they may not be able to see the cause of the trouble. Therefore your thought radiated clearly and wisely, especially when requesting the kind of help needed, is a very good form of prayer.

Why is the world filled with destruction, with sickness of the mind and body?

It is because your peoples do not learn how to use their powers of thought correctly. They think thoughts of hatefulness, heaviness and selfishness. You are spirits, radiant spirits, using your bodies in these few short years of your earthly life, but what do you do with your radiant power which the Master Creator has invested in you? You surround yourselves with feeble thoughts of self-pity, with the tattered garments of pride, and only occasionally are we able to draw aside the curtains of your pretence and self-pity that for a little while you may peer out like frightened children and behold the truth, the truth that you are creative spirits living here in your mortal world, yet afraid to create.

When you let go your garments of negativity and come forth to stand in the knowledge that you are spirits using a body, filled with the same creative power and energy which we of the spirit are able to use, then indeed can you begin to create new patterns of hopefulness, joy and truth, which will fill your world with beauty and enclothe you each one with radiant colour and light. Every thought is creative, every negative thought is creative, and because this is true you destroy yourselves and each other, and quietly you destroy the beauty of the world.

You destroy when you think jealously or hatefully, for out of your consciousness there goes a creation which is barbed and poisonous, piercing the sensitive aura of that one of whom you think, but if they refuse to accept your thought, it circles round and round, then returns to you, and unto yourself will come the destruction. You may think your thoughts are unknown to those surrounding you, but we can see with the vision of spirit, and we rejoice when we behold the inward struggle within some souls as they slowly try to eliminate the old negative thoughts to replace them with positive thoughts of hope, creativeness, health and love, and so we behold the spiritual being beginning to shine with the mystic beauty of spiritual light.

When we form a question in our minds and receive the answer by thought, does it come from those in charge of us or are we able to tap the higher consciousness?

The answer is invariably transmitted from the consciousness of the spirits who are watching over you, but in the evolvement of the higher forms of mediumship it is possible to receive directly from certain sources either wisdom, answers to questions, or inspiration in the form of music or art.

How do we know where the answer comes from?

When you receive information directly from the Central Source you will be aware of an intensely alert state of mind, a tremendous quietness, and sometimes a sense of light gathering around you. But when your mind is full of turmoil and the answers to questions come in the form of symbols or strong impressions, then it has come from a mind which understands your mind.

How can we contact higher spheres so we may always be able to distinguish clearly the right course from the wrong?

Be still. Eliminate all desire. Think of a still pool in which is reflected clearly every leaf and branch of the trees encircling it. That symbolises your mind reflecting the great truth which is above. But if in the pool a fish breaks the surface of the water, disturbing the image of the trees, then it is no longer true. So it is with you if you allow some earthly desire, some lower thought, to break the stillness.

Can perfect physical health be gained by the power of thought?

No, not by the power of thought, but it can be gained by the purification of thought, so that the mental body comes into complete harmony with the spirit which is trying to express itself through the thought and emotional bodies. Each of you is gaining experience of controlling these vehicles, and through this you confront the multiplicities of life and resolve them into simplicity.

One simple method to attainment of harmony is to cultivate the habit of non-action. Refrain as much as possible from giving forth any reaction into the outer world until you have paused to analyse that which has taken place. When in your passage along a street, although the pavement is nearly empty another walks straight into you, your first reaction will be to say: "This man is not looking where he is going, therefore I have the right to be annoyed with him." But if you follow the policy of non-action, then you will think, "Was he drawn to me by a ray of attraction, and have I a service to render unto him?" This would be a policy of non-action by you, giving time to consider that which had occurred. So, in all similar incidents of the day. Your spirit, as onlooker, viewing the whole phase of life, stands and considers it before any reaction occurs within the mind or feeling.

In such a fashion your reaction must be a spiritual one.

CHAPTER FIVE

Approaches to Meditation

Regarding the need for prayer and meditation, can you suggest ways by which we might rise above the many things which hold us to the earth?

By establishing within yourself the habit of prayer and quiet remembrance, such as has been created in many religious communities, in which at every hour a bell is rung, bringing back the community to the recollection of God. You may appoint for yourself a time at a certain hour when, whatsoever you are doing, as soon as your eye sees that time automatically you will re-establish your remembrance of the power, unity and beauty of the most High. You do not need to pause in your occupation. Some people can establish this each time they see a child, some at morning and evening. It is an individual pattern created by simply switching your consciousness from its awareness of what you are doing unto the remembrance of the power and majesty of God. You may also sit quietly in meditation for a short time, watching the rhythm of your breath, breathing in life and breathing out love, for life and love are the very essence of the Universal Spirit itself. Having established this habit you will discover peace.

I find it difficult to break the chains of comfort. I try to meditate a night, but sleep always overcomes me.

It is easier for the soul to unfold and for the spirit to grow when it has less of the comforts of civilisation. If you wish to scale the spiritual heights then must you discipline the body and the bodily desires, applying yourself to the gaining of spiritual treasure with the same assiduousness as you give to the gaining of earthly treasure or wealth. The gifts of the spirit are not given; they are gained! The ways of the spirit are taught and shown, but only you can walk upon the ways, and only you can practise what we teach.

The treasures of the soul which you may attain in your high moments of spiritual enlightenment are more beautiful, more precious than any you can gain in your places of bodily comfort. So seek, pray, and establish rhythm in your lives, and discover for yourself the beauty of the spirit and the richness of the soul.

How can one remain peaceful and unruffled?

Try to hold within some place in your mind a simple word. You may hold fast unto the word "Jesu" or to a simple symbol such as a cross. In the midst of your busy activity let your mind revert to this one word. Or in conversation you may be listening to another but your mind can rest on the thought, "Peace, peace, peace," so that it becomes a note sounding in the inward places of your consciousness.

You have a mind that recollects many things, so as your conscious mind repeats this word it is like an echo which the mind of recollection brings forth in response. So, although you may be hurried or weary, the inward sounding word brings up from the wells of memory, peace, peace.

When the earthly mind seems to be predominating in one's meditation time, is it helpful to use music?

Truly, for as the sound of music goes forth into the atmosphere surrounding you in colour and beauty, it vibrates upon the delicate unfolding spiritual consciousness and will often bring it into peace. It also brings relaxation to the mortal body itself, and as the body relaxes so it comes into harmony with the spirit. In your world too little is known about radiations of sound and their reaction upon the delicate structures of the mortal body as well as those of the spiritual body.

When one wishes to meditate and does not feel well, is it better to leave it, or perhaps to try as best one can?

It is better to leave the effort at meditating, but to spend a short time in affirming or recollecting the quality of meditation. In other words, lie upon your bed to rest and renew your strength, but as it is your accustomed time for meditation, remember this, and in your recollection go back in thought to a moment when you experienced the full beauty of a previous one. By doing this you re-establish a link with the influence of that previous time.

Could it be said that until one has learned to concentrate properly and single-mindedness is achieved, one is not ready to meditate?

That is true, because in your everyday training the mind is not taught either to meditate or to concentrate. The child in school is taught to switch the mind from one subject to another so there is a multiplicity of thoughts imparted to the mind, and when the child reaches adulthood there is still this same tendency for many interests to gain the attention of the mortal mind.

Would you say, then, that in training oneself to concentrate one should do only a single thing?

Yes, for often the fingers may be occupied in a labour and the mind may be somewhere else.

So we have to learn to concentrate upon these mundane things which we really do not like doing in order to reach the goal?

Yes. A soul taking its way through the seasons of the mortal life should undertake its work with a full degree of knowledge that *everything* it does is important, if it is charged with the spirit of love and with awareness that this is a spiritual opportunity. The paper you touch, the pen you hold, the thought you think, all become impregnated with the great universal life-power of light, truth and beauty, once you are aware that you are a spirit, part of the great Eternal Spirit.

When one concentrates on a particular job of work in the daily life to such a degree that there is only a slight awareness of what is happening around, is that what you mean?

Truly. And just such concentration is needed, so that as you enter into meditation your mind may easily concentrate upon the subject of your meditation, and through that come swiftly into peace. You can then take a further step and meditate upon the thought of a candle burning within a still place, and as your thought comes through that still flame, you may enter into deeper stillness and come to greater knowledge.

What are the first steps to meditation?

There are many ways, for it means bringing the mortal mind into harmony with the spiritual mind that the two may blend.

So you may meditate while seated upon a quiet hillside or within a garden, trying to blend your mortal mind with the stillness and peace of the great realm of nature, as your thoughts cease the busyness of their activity and come into a slower rhythm, until at last the rhythm of thought itself dies away and you are at peace.

In your desire for spiritual unfoldment seek for the habit of meditation, that at any moment you may stop, be still and at peace. Then the mortal mind feels the peace of the great oversoul, the spiritual mind, interpenetrating it so that the two become one in harmony and joy. True melody is created by a vibration of notes, then a pause, a note, then a pause. When you sing, your voice rises then drops down and rests, and out of your resting and rising is melody. Whether music comes from your own throat and lips or the flowing of singing streams, still it is created as much by the resting as by the sounding of notes and singing.

Human existence is a sounding forth of notes, a melody, and each of you are part of the whole symphony of life. Therefore your soul needs to sing, then to rest and pause, to wait and be still, that within its resting it may take up new vibrations: the thousand things you each undertake day by day.

Do your earthly work, speak your many words, but establish a rhythm in your life of quiet pausing, of coming into peace. Slacken the tension for a moment and remember you are spirit; for a second you are at peace. In that second the mortal mind becomes renewed and refreshed as it is tuned unto the overself. The habit of meditative recollection when established regularly and rhythmically in your daily life will mean that easily and safely you may go into the deeper silence. Here the mortal mind may be released from the pressure of duty thoughts and be allowed to relax in the beauty thoughts of the spirit, for often duty brings strain, but beauty brings relaxation and harmony.

When meditating, is it good always to concentrate on the same theme or symbol?

It is good to use the same seed thought for a period, but to change it occasionally, for the mortal mind becomes automatic in its reaction to certain things, and a change of the seed idea for a few weeks is profitable.

You were speaking about tuning in to the natural forces. Is it possible while meditating to hear the sound of a particular flower? Some people say they hear wheat singing or bluebells ringing.

Yes, if persevered with, you will find that as you begin to seek for that attunement and awareness a great new world of beautiful discovery opens before you.

When one sits for meditation, do the guides and spirit friends take any part?

The part that guides would play is to impinge upon your first efforts their peace or tranquillity, especially if you have been living in a state of emotional unrest or have not yet learned the first lesson of concentration. Within the spirit realm there is a large body of ministering spirits who in their mortal lives were nuns, monks, hermits or yogis, under the guidance of those who knew the pathway of meditation, concentration and contemplation. So when a soul such as yourself desires to meditate and takes the first steps towards the lighting of the candle flame of clear meditative thought, a light or sound will vibrate into the inner planes. To you will be attracted a spirit who understands your weakness, your lack of development, and who will stand near to impart to your aura either the blueness of tranquillity, or to blend with your mind their steadiness in concentration. If there is a psychic weakness within the mediumistic body they will stand near to guard you from any invasion which may take place owing to your ignorance or misunderstanding of the laws you are seeking to apply. It is in this blending of the guide's consciousness with yours that you are slowly strengthened and brought from stage to stage of understanding, until at last you break through into the clear realisation of that which you are seeking. Then, their work completed, those who have been guiding you may withdraw to undertake the guidance of another upon a similar pathway.

Would it not be good for more people to learn to meditate in this very hectic life-style today?

Truly, for it would not only bring quietness to the mind and peace to tormented emotions, but this meditation of which I speak will open the way for true healing of the spirit to flow through. The outcome should be harmony of body, health and renewal of body forces, peace of mind and control over emotions. If you do not achieve these from your meditation, then you need to learn again, to be persistent, until the inflow of peace, life and love rejuvenates the physical and mortal body which is the instrument of the soul.

Does it help to wear a yellow garment for meditation?

It is a very good practice, for the yellow garment tends to quieten the mental activities and bring to constructive activity the power of the intellect, but make it of a delicate primrose colour, or wear a garment which has an embroidery of pure gold upon it.

When you speak of people wearing gold, does that apply to everyone?

It applies to those who are aspiring towards spiritual development and to an understanding of spiritual matters, those who earnestly desire to use their minds to understand the laws by which life is governed by the great Master Creator, and to meditate in peace. It is also for those who try to express their understanding upon rays of inspiration, both spoken and in the form of music or art, for them, too, the golden light is indeed needed, as it replenishes and quickens the faculties of the brain cells when the brain appears to be tiring under a period of prolonged strain.

Does the sign of the cross serve any useful purpose?

It serves a very useful purpose so long as the person who is making such a sign is aware that they have spiritual power within themselves.

How can we use it in ordinary life?

At the closure of your day, spend a little time in the secrecy of prayer and meditation, and try to send forth into the air the shape of a shining cross, sending it upward through the roof of the home wherein you dwell into that part of the world nearest to you.

In your loving thought try to uphold it for a few moments above the roof of your house, and as you uphold it, those in the spirit who are working with you will draw near to invest this spiritual symbol with their own radiance and understanding, that the cross may be supported. During the hours of darkness it will be a light unto those who may suddenly lose the use of their physical bodies, for seeing the light of the cross which you have raised, they may find their way through the shadows towards it, and those ministering spirits who cluster around the cross may lift these recently dead ones into that radiance and safely bring them into the places of peace.

Would this only be of use to Christians?

In your world there are many men and women whose minds are clouded with fear, hate and confusion, and they know not what to believe or where to turn, because their faith in the goodness of the great Master Creator is destroyed by the many challenges and negative forces at work in your mortal world. This symbol of the cross is a sign known unto most of earth's children, whether they be born into the Christian or other faiths. They know that the cross is the symbol of compassion, and where the cross shines, therein goodness and compassion may be found.

Though only a small thing, nevertheless it is a message you are writing with the living power of your own inward soul as you seek to raise the cross, creating it by thought, sustaining it by will, and investing it with light as you think upon it at the closure of each day.

What is the difference between contemplation and meditation?

Contemplation is a quietness of the soul in which all activity has ceased and the soul is in a complete state of acquiescence, or meditation, in that it can only gaze, absorb or become absorbed into that which it is contemplating. There is no exact division between these three things, because they interblend and it is possible for the soul who becomes proficient to pass swiftly from concentration to meditation, and from this into contemplation, so the three become as one.

When one is contemplating some aspect of God and you become at rest, then God takes over in that silence. Isn't that contemplation?

I think you are symbolising in a differing measure that which I have tried to explain, for as you contemplate or become absorbed into, does not the thing in which you have become absorbed also absorb you?

In meditation, when the point is reached when one is not conscious at all, "just gone away," then you "return" refreshed, what should be done? Should one strive to retain some idea of the meditation?

No, for when you reach this stage you have reached the first degree of contemplation; you have entered into the deep state of silence and rest, to the degree that you become unconscious of the activity of the mortal body. In this state you have absorbed from the Universal God Spirit some aspect of life, love or renewal, so that when you return you are refreshed. Just give yourself more and more to this and you will get greater and greater refreshment.

First concentration, then meditation. What is ecstacy?

Ecstacy is that which is often experienced when the soul has managed to break through the confines of the mortal thought and has entered into unity with the universal state of consciousness which lies without. This may sometimes bring great peace or it may be known as a great love; it may come in a tremendous inflow of joy. This is symbolised by the word ecstacy.

From what you have said, could that be the moment when one is entranced or controlled?

No, this has no relationship whatsoever to the control of spirits over their mediums. It can only be undertaken by the seeking soul who realises itself as a spirit using its bodies for a season for experience in the mortal world, and desiring to attain to its own true self consciousness and unity with the source from which it has sprung.

The trance and joy which occurs through mediumship is something that we of the spirit can impart to mediums that they may be encouraged to seek for further development, greater knowledge.

Can you speak about the states of ecstacy experienced by people like St Teresa? What exactly is that?

It is the cleansing of the whole consciousness, so that it comes into a state of complete unity. Too often in the seeking after the things of spirit the spiritual consciousness is cleansed but the mortal or memory consciousness is still filled with fears and discords of the past. Therefore, persons such as those of whom you speak may spend long seasons in prayer and meditation, seeking to purify the deep hidden consciousness so that when the spiritual mind reaches out into unity with the power of God, then the joy which comes with such a union is translated not only to the spiritual mind, but also to the deeper subconscious mind so the whole person becomes radiated with the joy of the great Master Creator.

Would this spiritual cleansing account for the stigmata phenomenon experienced by some saints?

Yes, for in the particular cases of which you speak the individuals have dwelled in deep thought upon the aspects of the crucifixion and have in meditation tried to visualise what this has meant, so the subconscious becomes deeply impressed with these images. In the time of purification the images are brought to the surface and may reflect themselves in just this fashion. Any sincere individual, having a reverence for a particular symbol and dwelling in thought upon it may, when complete unity arises within the consciousness, show a sign of the symbol either upon their living flesh or in some part of the bodily self.

Is it possible to induce that by self-hypnosis?

Each of you do this, knowingly or unknowingly in your daily life, for you are filled with the images of age and weakness, and this thought sinks deep down into the inward consciousness until one day it is out-pictured upon the living flesh as old age. Those who visualise health and youth and the influence of spirit have this image deeply etched within the consciousness, and so the bodily form reflects the youthfulness of the spirit.

CHAPTER SIX

Understanding Mediumship

Can you give us some thoughts which may help in the unfoldment of mediumship?

As a spirit, it is difficult for me to fully appreciate the many harsh noises and vibrations which fill your world today. One of the first things an intending medium should cultivate is the ability to clear the mind of the many impressions that it gathers from day to day, so that you come to us of the spirit or into your circles of communication with a mind that is like a slate wiped clear of all previous impressions. But you do not do this. You come with all the pressing memories and problems of your daily life.

In the ancient temples, those training for mediumship learned to relax the very cells of the physical brain by an effort of will and mind by an effort of thought. You, too, can do this by understanding how to move the muscular structure of your face and head, how to control the action of your ears and jaw. You should learn how to move the muscles of your brow and back of the head so that by concentration you may relax any tension in your brain or skull. Truly, if you practise this then you will be learning one of the lessons in mastery—how to master yourself.

The development of a true and perfect mediumship should go hand in hand with this self-mastery. Therefore, after relaxing the body and brain bring the mental activities into stillness.

In the old temples, the priests and priestesses who were mediums and seers taught the importance of movements which you know as dance. As the hands were raised and lowered so there was an effect upon the spine, releasing pressures. Similarly with the fluidic backward and forwards movements of the body, which were designed to free the interlocking joints of the spinal column, the related nerves, and the ethereal flow of the spiritual force through the soul body, which is so frequently inhibited by tensions of the physical body. So do not be afraid to move: move with freedom and rhythm so that no tension can arise in your spine or brain. The first degrees of mediumship are in the development of perception which comes from a still mind and a receptive brain. So when you sit in relaxation, awaiting the calmness of the spirit to interpenetrate your mind, if you are free from tension you will find this easily accomplished.

In training the temple seers, initial development was brought about during the hours of rest and sleep. Mediums were taught to lie in a completely prone position upon their resting couches, their minds swept clear of all outward disturbance. Beside them would be a little pad of wax upon which, in the moment of waking, they could write words or memories they were able to bring back when the spirit was away from the physical body. Because the mind and brain were so relaxed these memories could be brought back swiftly and easily. This was not the confused dream state that so many of you experience, but the gathering of information and knowledge from the regions of the spirit which would later be proved in its correctness or error, by the teacher in charge of the development of such a soul.

You yourselves might profit by that practice. You should occasionally lie down to sleep in a state of great peace, the body not overloaded with excess of food, having the spiritual intention of what you desire to learn, where you wish to go, to what spirit you would direct your thoughts. This would bring you further development and understanding, so that returning to your physical body you would cease to grope in uncertain fashion, sending out confused thoughts. Instead you would go forward in sureness and peace, knowing who is guiding and guarding you, understanding who is teaching you, not because you have been told by another, but because your own soul knows this is true.

The man or woman who is on the path of mastery becomes a "knower", and when you are a knower of truth then all your uncertainties vanish as clouds vanish before the light of the rising sun.

When you meet in little groups, combining your influence one with the other, then you should learn to extend your spiritual aura, that it may become wing-like, and your wings may enfold the others who are seated near you in a tenderness of protection and a radiance of light. As you extend your influence in this fashion you bring about an expansion of your own spiritual being, becoming more receptive to the influence of your guides and spirits who wish to blend their influence with yours. It is almost impossible for any spirit to enter the aura when it is closed with self-concern and self-desire, when you are only interested in your own development and of acquiring knowledge for yourself. But when you love and desire protection for those others who are there, then your aura unfolds, your wings are outspread, and your love encircles them. As your aura widens and becomes sensitive, we of the spirit may draw near and impart to you and through you the truths, power and healing which we wish to give to earth's children, and which you yourselves desire, that you may serve in beauty and usefulness.

One other thought. Learn to direct your attention to the region above your brow, for it is in this region that all true spiritual mediumship is to be found and unfolded.

Truly your world needs mediums who know how to co-operate with the spirits of light and healing—those who can raise their attention above the immediate things of the earthly plane of the spirit. So, aspire! Aspire unto that which is highest, truest and best.

Why do you allow mediums to become caught up in the confusions of this life? So often it seems because of their sensitivity they suffer more mental and emotional anguish than other people?

We have to allow this until you learn how to be responsible for your own mediumship. It is only from your hurts that you become wiser and follow the teaching that we seek to give you. When you learn to maintain your body upon food which is best for your mediumship, to drink pure fluids and breathe pure air; when you avoid loading your body with excesses of food which clog and soil its cellular texture. In other words, when you have learned to use your body as the tool of your mediumship, then we can go forward and perfect this sensitiveness of the soul. We can begin to blend our consciousness with yours to give to earth's children some guidance, a small part of our revelation of the truths they are so urgently needing.

Then your responsibility ceases, for you are not responsible for what your brothers and sisters may do with the revelation given through you. Your responsibility is to be a good tool, to transmit that which is given, then to leave it with them or with the wise watchers of spirit who may till the soil that has been prepared, water the seed that is sown, or bring to fulfilment that which has been started in spirit and in truth.

The use of a medium to us is not only in words that are spoken or visions that are shown, for the power we give through them is also needed by earth's children. Joy, simplicity, purity, these are transmitted together with a quickening magnetic life-giving force of healing.

We can do much to repair the ravages of our mediums' mortal bodies and restore harmony and peace to strained minds, but only if they will enter into peace and lie at rest, communing with the healing forces of nature, not allowing themselves to feel the ambitions of the earthly minds and the demands of the earthly people thrusting upon them until they forget the responsibility they have for their own minds, hearts and bodies.

When we ask for guidance about which path we should take or which way we should go, and a thought comes into our minds, how can we tell the difference between our own wishful thinking and the guides telling us which way to go?

You need to simplify your request. Many of earth's people try to send their requests to us as spirits, but it does not come as a simple single question, rather as a confused picture in which many queries are involved. So, do not sent a thought saying, "Which way should I go?" but instead say, "Should I follow this pathway?" In such a fashion you will simplify your question and it will reach your guardians more clearly. As you ask, wait in quietude, and there should come to you one swift reply which will be "yes" or "no". When you receive this you may follow that pathway.

To whom should we give our faithfulness and allegiance? Is our responsibility to spirit or to earth? Should the needs of people and tasks of the daily life always take precedence?

First, you must understand that as unfolding mediums you are Spirit, and all people amongst whom you live are spirits now, just as they will be Spirit when they come to the closure of the earthly life. Your responsibility is always to Spirit, both as it manifests through the earthly body and through your mediumship. Your responsibility as a medium is always to stand between, with one half of your aura blended with those who are of the spirit spiritual and the other blended with the spirit in the earth. Therefore as a medium you are a golden link in a great chain whose highest link is in the purest light and whose lowest link is in the heaviest state of earthly matter that you can comprehend.

As part of that golden chain you must be a clear, pure and balanced link within yourself, for if you break it there is no inter-communication taking place. So the first responsibility is always, again and again, unto yourself, to maintain health and strength within your body, and harmony of emotions within your heart, that your love may stream out, not in great tumults of emotional desire and unrest, but in a steady stream of tenderness. By so doing, you are not giving way to selfishness, but maintaining an instrument in the perfection of harmony and health.

Each medium should write within their mind this thought: "The tender heart, the sound body and the clear mind. This is the instrument of spirit." Because this is so, learn to seek the right companionships, those friendships which evoke within your heart a gentle, peaceful lovingness, who can exchange with you their own wisdom, whose auras blend with yours that your mediumship may be strengthened and enhanced.

But how are we to serve if we seek only those who strengthen our mediumship?

When you learn to guard your mediumship, then we are able to blend with you so perfectly you know when you have to go forth on a mission of mercy, or when we desire you to help your weaker brothers and sisters. But until you understand your responsibility you go this way and that, allowing yourselves to become involved in the confusion of other people's lives. Discrimination and understanding are the jewels you need to develop within your own soul, for then we are able to bring you impressions and visions saying, "Help this one, go here, go there," because out of the wise understanding of your mediumship you can evolve a strong and perfect link with us.

Does the standard of spiritual evolvement attained by the medium affect the quality of the message transmitted?

Truly, for the deeper the sense of honesty within the inner

consciousness of the mediums, the clearer or higher is the revelation given through them. There are some who limit their mediumship by personal pride or ambition: some are limited by greed, the desire for gain, and have not the strength to transmute this into the higher generosity of the spirit. Others are limited by fear of failure, or of weakness of the flesh, or they fear the criticism of humankind.

Often the consciousness may be cleared of these cruder imperfections of the earth, but that may not always carry their honesty on to the more subtle and spiritual planes. Thus the medium who is insufficiently honest to admit, "Today the spirit is not with me" or "I have not this awareness which other people think I should have." As each one goes forward, always the honesty needs to be transferred from the plane of the earth unto the inner plane. Mediums can only reveal truth to the degree in which they are truthful themselves.

If we are truly honest with each other, surely sometimes we will say things that may hurt those near to us?

Temper your honesty with love and your speaking with kindliness, for the wise man and woman may see the untruths and imperfections with the clear open vision of their honest understanding, but they need not go forth saying to others, "You are untruthful, you are unkind, you are soiled with the stains of sinfulness." The wise one knows when to be silent, when to speak, and how to cloak that speaking with kindly words which soften the words of truth.

Some of you have learned to be so honest with yourselves that you hate the shams, the untruths; you say you cannot bear the dishonesties in the world about you. But I would say to you; ask yourselves, have you developed with your honesty the love which comes from the Eternal Source in a tenderness of compassion and healing? Has this love touched your heart so that round the bright, clear, golden disc of your honesty there may be seen the outer ring of softening blue, the garment of compassionate love?

Further, when the mortal body is left behind, if the soul has balanced honesty of purpose with true compassion and kindliness then is it able to rise with wings, for the wing of love and the wing of honesty of purpose can help the soul to soar high and clear into the regions of the spirit, into the radiant lands of light.

Those of us who have only just begun on this pathway, how can we be of use?

You all have some degree of mediumship for you are all on the pathway of development. So as you go on your way, think consciously that you are drawing round yourself a cloak of protective spiritual power, and send out, day by day, light from the centre of your heart and light with the will of your thought. As you walk in your city streets amongst the crowds, pause and send out light, that darkness may be dispersed. As you come to the end of your time of prayers, send out light into the building wherein you dwell, that it may be filled with light and the greyness annihilated. As you leave your house dedicated to the work of spirit, send out light into the entrance to seal it, that the darkness may not enter in.

This is a little task which you may all accomplish in your own particular degree of mediumship, so will you help to guard the world against the encroachment of shadows, pushing back some of the threat of destruction and war.

Why are some spirits unable to communicate direct, but only by relaying a message through other spirits?

Sometimes a spirit who does not come close to the earth has been taken through the Halls of Forgetfulness so that painful memories may be washed away from the recollection. When that has happened, the spirit will sometimes prefer to remain in the sphere to which he has become accustomed rather than coming back into the mortal life which may restart an echo of old memories. One of the compassionate works undertaken in the realms of spirit is that of taking the soul who has been persecuted, burned, tortured or ill-treated through the grey mists of forgetfulness, that the pain of the experience may be washed away and they may be able to enter into the fullness of joy.

Is there any way of telling if the spirit guardian is with you prior to trance?

The way to discover this is by seeking to find the especial signals which your group of spirits will establish to tell you of their presence.

They may endeavour to show a little bright spot or disc of colour; some spirits will make their presence felt by creating a feeling as of a cool breath upon your face, or a particular warmth which may affect your face, brain or area of your body. Learn to recognise these signals.

How can an ordinary person, one not specially gifted psychically, best co-operate with spirit helpers and guides?

First, through the enlargement and purification of your soul body, your spiritual aura. By right loving of earth's creatures, men, women and children, so does the aura expand and grow with compassion. Out of right loving and compassionate living will be born prayer, for as you love and desire to help so you send forth thoughts and healing prayers for those whom you see in need. This prayer and compassion together, purifying and enlarging the spiritual body, automatically brings you conscious knowledge of the power of the spirit helpers. It makes you sensitive to the Great Unseen, and from this co-operation comes spiritual healing and spiritual wisdom.

So, consideration of the needs of others, love and compassion; this is the first step upon the way.

Many of us truly desire to be of service, but as we grow older it seems our greatest and hardest service is to stand back and let younger people take the more active role.

Yes, this is an aspect of earth experience which is not sufficiently understood. First, for each of you there should be seasons of growth and learning in which the body is developed and you are taught to live wisely. Then a time of responsibility for parents, partners and children, or to a social group, and through service unto these you gain strength and experience which carries you far forward to that period of life when you can sit back and allow others to continue the work and responsibility. Thus the soul should become a fountain of spiritual power through which wise and loving thoughts are directed into the lives of the surrounding people.

In years gone by this was well understood, but today it has been forgotten, and you have men and women in their latter years trying to lead lives of great activity instead of devoting this time of life to the quietness of prayer and meditation, and to the preparation for peacefully leaving the body and entering with wisdom the life of the spirit. You have the breakdown of ancient family ties which had great value, so that old people are no longer supported by those who should love them, but are languishing in lonely bitterness and fear.

At the dawning of your latter years, stand back and learn to use the power of thought more constructively, sending out thoughts of peace, harmony, healing and cleansing into the atmosphere. Spend a little while withdrawing from all the things which held your attention in your earlier years and open your mind to the spirit forces of beauty, wisdom and peace. Thus you will confirm more completely to the spiritual law.

When we sit for development, we are often told that a nun spirit is helping us. Why should this be so?

These holy spirits known to you as nuns, but to us as the dedicated white-robed sisters, continue here in the spirit life the work and service they began on earth. They choose to come back to blend with your hearts and minds qualities gained in their earthly experience, and in return they receive new understanding. Through remaining close they are aware of your inward thoughts and your struggles to overcome the weakness in your own nature.

First, they bring peace, the peace of a quietened mind, the peace of the soul. Then they bring discipline learned from an ordered life in which times were given unto prayer and meditation, and where tasks were conscientiously done every time. They bring also something of the power of the great Christ spirit. While on earth, through much prayer, thought and forward looking toward the Master Jesus they created the slender bridge of golden thought by which their hearts became attuned unto Him. On entering the spirit world these many nun souls pass swiftly through the first planes of spirit towards the one on whom their thoughts had been so firmly set—the Christ plane, which is charged with the heavenly love of the Master Jesus himself. Dwelling for a while in His presence they offer themselves unto Him and are sent forth unto the earth upon missions of mercy, love and service. Through the mediums they impart some vision of the beauty they have seen, of the light absorbed, of the love so needed in the earth. Because they have this understanding and have been enchristed within the Christly realm, they can draw around you the protective mantle of their spiritual light, imparting the simplicity, lovingness and joy inherent in their own soul self.

How can we avoid feeling suddenly depleted of energy and exhausted by the jangling elements of daily life?

As you breathe forth your ancient prayer saying, "Give us this day our daily bread," you think only that the bread must feed the cellular structure of the body itself so that it may be a strong tool for the use of the spirit. But as you begin to develop, so the energies of your bodies become active upon higher and higher spiritual planes, and sustenance is needed not only from the earth but from the ethers surrounding the earth—the food of thought, of the heart, and eventually food of the spirit.

Your prayer must incorporate the asking for kindred companions that your heart may blend with the stream of love flowing from another heart, and you need the food of thought, the exchange of ideas between minds alert to the inspiration blowing from the spirit realm like a freshening breeze, otherwise the mind will become starved, stultified, and part of the unfolding spiritual being will fall sick. As this harmony of mind, heart and body unfolds there comes an awakening and expansion of the spiritual aura itself, and this needs the food of the soul—the energised rays of the sun which move through the ethers of your earth in the dawn and evening hours. You should walk in these quiet times, inbreathing through your quickening etheric body the fine subtle energy, for the sun's rays strike the earth at a different angle to that during the day. This is the food of the inner soul which will reflect back into the outward body. There comes yet another development upon a still higher plane, for the spirit itself needs the food that is gathered in the silence of meditation and spiritual communion.

Therefore, take this key of knowledge, go forth to meet other men and women and listen to their hearts, read the messages within their eyes, and there you will see what is their true need. For some it will be the food of thought or of love, to recreate harmony, others need to inbreathe the etheric energies, while some need to learn how to receive in the inward quietude of meditation and prayer the food of the spirit.

Why are we sometimes very aware of the power of the spirit while at other times it seems so removed and distant?

There is no mystery in this. You need only understand that you have two differing states of consciousness, an earthly mind and a spiritual mind. In your development you are seeking to create a more complete bridge between the two, so that you may consciously use the spiritual mind and consciously and willingly quieten the earthly mind. Because this material mind is concerned with worldly things such as the pursuits of the day, the customs of the society in which you live, there is a tendency to believe that it is all-important and that the body is all that exists; so when the spiritual mind becomes active the earthly mind is confounded and confused because it cannot understand and explain that which is of the spirit, spiritual. When you meditate you are trying to use the spiritual mind to gain control over the earthly mind and bring the two into complete harmony.

How can we become more attuned to the guardians and guiding ones?

Lift up your thoughts and love unto them, for the awareness of things of the spirit—the spiritual consciousness—takes place above the brow line of the brain, but the earthly consciousness is in a line level with and below the area of the human brow. Surely it is not hard to think in the higher area of your brain, to lift your thought from the area of your chin to your crown, for in this practice is contained the essential understanding of unfoldment and mediumship. You need to wear your crown of spiritual unfoldment symbolised by the shining light within the upper part of the spiritual aura. The spiritual mind absorbs the atmosphere of spirituality as a sponge absorbs moisture; beauty, power and knowledge that has been absorbed in this way filters through into the more active everyday awareness and you will say you feel refreshed and enfolded in deep peace.

Therefore, day by day, sit in quietude with the mortal mind at rest, then let attention rise slowly upward to the eyebrows, upward into the higher regions of the brain that the spiritual mind may release its store of wisdom and beauty into the material mind. In this peace those of the spirit who guide and love you may draw near to drop into the quietened spiritual mind their own thoughts, visions or words. Open yourself to spiritual influence, let that mind be active that the mortal mind may receive its blessing, then direct your thought unto the Master Creator in thanks. In this way your unfoldment will come in ever-growing expanding circles of radiant light.

When one sits for meditation, do the guides or spirit friends take any part?

The guides impinge their peace or tranquillity upon your first efforts, especially if you have been living in a state of emotional unrest or have not yet learned the first lesson of concentration.

Within the spirit realm there is a large body of ministering spirits who in their mortal lives were nuns, monks, hermits or yogis, under the guidance of those who knew the pathway of meditation. So when a soul such as yourself desires to meditate and takes the first steps toward lighting the candle flame of clear meditative thought, a sound will vibrate into the inner planes and a spirit will be attracted to you, one who understands your weaknesses, your lack of development, and who may stand near to impart to your aura the blueness of their tranquillity, or to blend with your mind their steadiness in concentration.

If there is a psychic weakness within the mediumistic body they stand near to guard you from any invasion which may take place owing to your ignorance or misunderstanding of the laws you are seeking to apply. It is in this blending of the guide's consciousness with yours that you are slowly strengthened until at last you break through into the clear realisation of that which you are seeking. Then, their work completed, those who have been guiding you may withdraw to undertake the guidance of another upon a similar pathway.

CHAPTER SEVEN

Restoration of Harmony

I am not a healer, but I often wish I could help people who need healing. What can I do?

If you have sufficient understanding that you yourself are a spirit, then you can draw upon the spiritual power which is forever at work in the world.

If you desire to draw healing to yourself or to impart it to others who are in need, seat yourself in some restful place and allow to drop away all fret, anxiety and fear, slowly bringing yourself into a state of quiet meditative thought until you are conscious of the deep peace of the spirit and the warm power of the Love which heals all things. Then in loving thought send to those you desire to help the silver thread of your influence. Visualise their eyes as you last saw them, for the eye is the window of the soul, and if the expression of the eye was weary, lonely or closed with fearfulness, see it changed into joy, peace and glowing health. Try to hold that picture, at the same time attempting to unite these people whom you desire to help with the flowing warmth and peace which is coming to you.

Always where there is a desire to help there will be the watching spirits who will endeavour to forward your work. Spiritual healing is very much a living influence transmitted from soul to soul, and it will flow from your soul into theirs.

Many people seek healing going from one healer to another, but they fail to get better. Why?

It would be better if they would seek firstly with honesty within themselves to discover *why* they are ill and do not improve. Truly, some sicknesses are not healed by the healers because the inner consciousness of the patient desires to keep this sickness as a shield against their inner state of inadequacy. Truthfulness of the spirit should bring its own reward, so long as there is honesty of purpose between patient and healer.

Are there any limitations to spiritual healing? I am thinking of epidemics. Could such illness be avoided?

There are no limitations to the power of the spirit. There is a community consciousness, and almost without their awareness people may become influenced by the waves of fearful thought which are emanated by the nation or group which is surrounding them, and it needs a high degree of spiritual enlightenment to withstand these.

When you absorb such thought vibrations of fear or disharmony you become part of the whole sea of infectious disease, but if you are steadfast in daily indrawing the power of Light and breathing out healing and harmony to those around you, then you can cancel this negative community power of thought and keep yourself and the people near you in harmony and freedom from disease.

Can one become a more efficient instrument for healing by trying to think of one's healing guide, or is it better just to think of something spiritual?

It is better to try to empty yourself more completely so that you become a clearer channel, an empty vessel. Because you have the desire to heal, so you are known as a healing vessel, and as you give yourself to your healing work, try to let go from yourself all anxiety and strain, bringing yourself into a state of relaxation. Simply hold the thought, "Here am I, a vessel which must be filled because I am trying to empty myself." Thus you should find the healing ray come in greater strength and purity.

One way to do this is to place your hand upon the one who is sick, relax yourself in body and mind and simply hold within your consciousness a thought that the power of the healer and patient are one. Unite yourself with the power so that without effort, striving or strain there is unity between the power, the patient and yourself.

Why cannot you heal people upon earth without our help?

In some cases we are able to bring renewing spiritual energy direct unto the sick person, but often the renewing force they need is of the etheric realm, and therefore the healer transmitting spiritual energy is also transmitting force which is within the living ether of your earth.

It could be symbolised in this fashion: if you took a fish from the water and it lay dying upon the earth, I could give the fish renewing life force, but unless you returned the fish into the water it would die, for it needs not a superabundance of air, it needs air diluted, which it gets within the water. Even so, the human being is sick because there is a lack of etheric life-force pulsating through the etheric body. We may bring a renewal of spiritual energy unto that person, but if they cannot gather sufficient etheric life force then the spirit will be strengthened and renewed but the etheric body will not, and so death may take place. Thus the loved one will come in strength into the spirit life, but will not remain in strength here upon your earth.

Why do we sometimes feel the spiritual power strongly, while at other times hardly at all? How can we best harness it for the good of others?

There is no increase in the power, only in your capacity to receive, contain and to channel it through your own personality into the earthly experience. You need to learn how to be harmonious channels, not by making great and sweeping changes in yourselves, but in knowing how to conserve your own natural energies and to use them wisely.

Consider the young children in your midst; do they not reflect tremendous activity as they run, jump, speak and move? They have not yet learned an essential lesson, that the great flowing flux of life has to be controlled and used harmoniously if it is to bring harmony and beauty into being. So you say unto them, "You must learn to rest, to sleep and to be still, that you many not tire yourselves needlessly." But you do not go far enough, you fail to teach them how to conserve their energies that they may enter into the inwardness of silence.

Your hours of loneliness are precious gifts granted unto you, but how often do you use them wisely? You fritter the hours away in useless occupations instead of bringing the body and mind under the subjection of the will, that you may conserve the spiritual energy of the soul and mind, and the healthful energy of the body. How often, too, you dissipate energy in your speaking together. This is good when it is the expression of your love and desire to understand each other, but how much energy is fruitlessly dissipated in pointless remarks, in what you call "polite conversation"? The voice can heal, the tongue can bless. Truly, your words can bring beauty and harmony unto the earth when they are the outward sounding forth of the spiritual energy flowing from your inward consciousness.

This is the secret of your power: learning how to speak and when not to speak; learning how to control your thoughts so that gradually they become ideas of idealism, lovingness and truth. Eliminate thoughts which vibrate round and round yourself in self-concern, in fear of the future or regret over the past. These serve no purpose except to exhaust you so that when you desire to bring forth healing, you say, "I do not know why it is, but the power is weakened today." It is not the power which is weakened, but it is your inability to receive, to conserve and to respond.

Truly the spiritual life is one of discipline and service, the golden joy of service, but you may only attain unto the fullness when you are in harmony with the great flowing Divine spiritual power.

So, seat yourselves in peace, think upon the things eternal, and conserve within yourselves the energies of life.

Is it possible to conserve healing force?

From your hands flows a spiritual magnetism, and this usually can be seen in rays of blue, either dark or pale blue, and when the fingers are curled, then is the blue radiance turned in upon itself so that a blue globe is created there. Meditate upon this, because it is the blue globe of healing which later you will use.

When you desire to prepare yourself for healing or helping another, sometimes fold over your fingers and close within your hands the spiritual force of your own spirit, then, when you give your hands in healing and comradeship to another, it is transmitted to them in life and beauty.

Why does one sometimes feel very weary and depleted when helping people?

This is because you are allowing them to draw strength from you, rather than you yourself drawing strength from above and sending it forth to them in a conscious effort of love and thought. So long as you keep your attention turned upward toward the great canopy of spiritual power, allowing this to flow into yourself, you can send out light and love in feeling and thought without becoming unduly exhausted. But if you are trying to carry those who are weak, or allowing them to extract energy from you, then you are not living in harmony with spiritual law.

The spiritual law is: draw the power and give it forth, and in this you cannot be exhausted.

Does meat-eating affect healing power?

I think the eating of meat will make little difference to the healing power you are using so long as your state of consciousness is not identified in pleasure with the food you eat. The sustenance of the mortal body should always be taken with detachment, and with the thought that, as you partake of food, it is the offering of the low and mortal self unto the high and immortal self, that it may be translated into the energy needed for this particular work. If you load your body with too much animal food you may upset the chemical balance, and this will interfere with the flow of healing force, but if it is only a small amount and your spiritual consciousness is correct, then it would make but little difference.

How can absent healing help ease great pain?

Do not send forth the thought concerned with the easing of pain, but rather think of an instrument in which the strings have been tightly bound so they are taut and vibrating with too strong a vibration. Visualise those strings being tuned, slackened, so that as the hand of the harpist goes across them it may vibrate melody and harmony, not the discordancy of broken strings. Much pain of the physical body is the result of nerves which are taut and tight with fear.

How does absent healing work?

The healers transmit healing energy. They sit together in silence so that their spiritual consciousness may be raised. As they attune themselves unto the spiritually potent etheric force this flows into them, charging their spiritual and etheric body with a super-abundance of energy. Then from within their etheric body comes a silvery thread of light which is joined to the sick person, and through this fine thread of light is transmitted the increased abundance of spiritual energy. The patient's spiritual body is stimulated and recharged, and the etheric body is brought back again into an abundance of energy so that the disease force disappears and is replaced by health and harmony.

Is it ever a kind of psychic interference to send out love and healing to someone who has not asked for it?

No, for if you are sending love and healing winged with compassion this cannot harm another soul. It will soothe or enrich. But if that one is truly resistent to that which you are extending, then what has been sent will not be accepted and may circle round and return to yourself. You can never cause harm by giving forth love and by endeavouring to create harmony.

How can a person be helped after suffering a stroke which results in the lost use of part of their body, for example, an arm or leg? What is the cause?

What you call a stroke is the result of thickening of blood causing some congestion or injury within the brain. The reason for this often lies in the emotional body, for where there are extremes of anger or poor control over the emotions, the delicate heart centre is affected, and eventually there is congestion of the blood resulting in this injury to the brain. So there are two conditions here, one belonging to the spiritual being, one to the physical body. I would say that the immobilisation of the leg, arm, or organs of speech simply results in the slight stagnation in the flow of energies within the ethereal body. But if there is an outpouring of healing energies from an attendant healer, often this will stimulate the dormant energies in the spiritual being, and may also clear the damage which has occurred in the physical brain. Then, if there is a calming and healing within the emotional body, some movement and renewal of health can be regained.

Does it matter if a patient is non-co-operative in absent healing?

No, for upon the spiritual level thought is creative and thought is energy, therefore the healer can send thought and energy to a link such as yourself. As you think lovingly of the patient, you receive the living force from the healer and transmit it to the loved one.

Try to understand that on the spiritual level, *all thought is energy and energy is creative,* and in this great etheric stream of life around you, there is nothing which can hinder it if it is sent with love and spiritual intent.

How can I heal myself?

You should endeavour to spend time, day by day, in the remembrance of the source from which you have sprung. You are spirit, spirit using your body, so your body is only the tool of your spirit. If you gain a purer, clearer spirit consciousness of the Master Creator, then you attune yourself to this perfect power and it will harmonise and heal the body, restoring it to health.

I know a vicar's wife whose hands are twisted with arthritis, but who is always joyful and uncomplaining. Why has she this affliction?

I would say that such a soul has deep within her spiritual self certain faculties either for art or music, or even for the religious life, which in her inner self she desires to express, but because the pattern of her earthly life labours have to be fulfilled, responsibilities carried, and the outward formalities of religion observed: all these fill her days. So instead of blessing her hands, she may create a barrier between the inward flowing desire of the soul and that daily toil which has to be outwardly expressed through the mortal body. This would create a blockage between the spiritual will and the use of the hands.

Are some individuals in tune with certain plants or trees?

Truly, for each plant and tree has its own healing vibration, and a note of power is sounded by all plants and trees within the framework of that pattern. Persons who are in need of a particular harmonising force, by cultivating certain plants or by attuning themselves unto a woodland or walking within a forest, may find that the vibratory note plays upon them. Through their attunement they gain harmony and healing.

How would they realise it?

By a feeling of harmony. Restoration takes place first within the spiritual bodies, but truly mediumistic people may become aware of a note or melody emanating from a group of trees or plants.

Does that account for flowers thriving better in some rooms or houses?

Yes, but where living persons are in a state of disharmony, then as the plant or flower vibrates its essential keynote of harmony, this disharmonious one may absorb it to such a degree that the plant, deprived of its harmonising force, will die before its ordinary season of existence is completed.

If physical affliction is a conscious choice of the soul before incarnation, is it right to try to heal the affliction?

Truly, for healing is the expression of love. Love is the power which cleanses, forgives and understands. Therefore, although there may be some souls who enter the earthly life to undertake the difficult experience of pain or bodily imperfection because of something they desire to learn, there is no reason why their pain should not be eased by love, nor yet the debt cancelled and cleansed by the higher love force expressed through healing. Indeed, quite often a sufferer may be brought into contact with a healer that the law may work in such a fashion when they are almost ready to be healed.

Much of this teaching of karma is only partly understood and expressed in your world, for this sense of debt and this feeling of the need to suffer is often only in the consciousness of the incarnating soul; it is not a burden laid upon that one by some external power. Therefore, if that soul can become aware of the cleansing and forgiving love it will be cleansed of its own self-punishment.

What happens when an apparently dying person is healed?

Each spirit entering into the mortal existence forms a chain of life. Within this chain are years and months of experience. Even as a chain has its weaker and strong links, so each spirit having within its use this chain of life, chooses to live sometimes for sixty years, maybe for a season of one hundred years or even for three years. So we look to see whether it is good and right to strengthen the hold of a spirit upon its body by looking on the whole chain. If the illness is simply associated with the weakening of the link, then we will strengthen it so that life and inspiration may continue. But if the chain ceases, then we say, "This is the time when this beloved one has chosen to leave the mortal existence," and we will help their leaving of the body and coming into spirit.

What part of a tree should we use for healing?

This will depend upon your purpose. If your natural energies have become lowered and you feel exhausted, then stand against a tree. Lean your back against it so that the sensitive nerves and the etheric flow in your spine may be re-energised from the energy forces which flow up and down through the etheric body of the tree.

If you wish to make healing foods or drinks, then it is good to use the flowers, sometimes the leaf. Take from the lime tree its leaves and blooms and infuse these in water, then drink the liquid. It will clear the mind and strengthen the soul. Take from your strong oak tree part of the blossom, and in using this it will bring a degree of strength. The elder tree which bears great clusters of white blooms and in its turn, purple berries, is especially beneficial to those who are older. The flower, leaf and berry have qualities very helpful to those weakened by the slowing down of the body cells through advancing years.

How can we attune ourselves to the rhythms of the earth in order to remain well and happy?

As the winter ends and the first signs of spring manifest, each man and woman should say: "Now I will give my body a period of rest, in preparation for the rising tide of life." For two or three days you should withdraw from normal activities and rest and fast, allowing extra cleansing to take place in the cells of the body. After this, go forth and attune yourself to the rhythm of the earth and you will feel you want to walk, to run, to be active, as the animating energy begins to surge in renewing power through your body.

If you are becoming spiritually aware, you will "feel" intuitively when this time is needed. You should allow this period of resting and renewal to govern your living, so at this time change your food from the warm clogging foods of winter to the lighter substances of the renewing spring. Eat the new young leaves as plants come into being. Make drinks from dried herbs and take honey which will give you energy in a new form by energising the cells of the body.

When autumn comes, attune yourself to the newer rhythm, feeding your body on nuts, seeds and berries—food which nature has provided for man in that season—so that your body may be carried forward on nature's own rhythm.

If you do this, you will find your spiritual consciousness will begin to tell what your body requires that it may be a good instrument, a centre through which you may manifest spiritually, in harmony and joy, without weakness or disease. Food should be the medicine of the body, and when your spiritual knowledge is strong, then indeed your medicine is in the natural foods.

It is difficult to find time to do these things with all the tension of life in the world today.

Yes, and it is for that reason I stress this thought that you should allow yourself a little season of rest for two or three days as the winter gives way to spring, so that you may *feel* the change in the rhythm and allow the body to have its "little death" followed by its "renewal of life". By so doing, much stress and illness can be prevented.

When we are attracted by a particular sound, is it one we have an affinity with, or something of which we are deficient?

When you listen to sound you should listen with your inner awareness, discovering in what area of your person the note brings forth an answering vibration. There should come, either underneath your heart or in the area of your brain, a response to that especial note, and as you respond to it so you will know that this is your keynote at this particular time. If you are aware within yourself that there is disharmony, then let that note sound and vibrate through you to bring about a reharmonisation of the atoms of the soul and body.

Many of you forget these ancient truths, the powers of intonation or incantation. As you intone through a number of notes your voice will eventually reach one which is easy and familiar to you. If you sound that note it should bring about a gradual re-organisation of the atoms within your being. It is one of the simple exercises practised by those who wish to heal by sound.

Is that the same as saying a mantra?

To say a mantra is surely to make an incantation, but it would be better to speak it, letting the sound vibrate from your inner self. If you sound a high note of joy, then you bring about healing in the higher areas of your person; if you sound it on the deeper notes, then the healing occurs in the lower part of your body.

You have spoken about the healing properties in sound vibration. Is there a scale of sound applicable to various illnesses?

This is a healing cult which will come into being as your world moves forward into the subtleties of the age which is still to come, for it will move out of the present methods of surgery into the harnessing of the power of light, sound and colour, to bring about healing and the restoration of health.

Sound is the primal stirring force which causes energy to congeal into atomic patterns which become the created world in the midst of which you dwell. But if you can harness sound to colour and then detect the colouration which is weak in the soul body of the one whom you desire to help, then often harmony can be restored by the simple vibrating of that sound. But this is a method which needs extreme carefulness in use, for continued sound can be destructive as well as constructive, and so we do not give the full token of understanding to earth's children concerning this until they have the wisdom to use it wisely.

But it is also true to say that in your world you have simple songs and hymns which have a harmonising effect upon the soul bodies of those who sing them, and to whom they are sung. These songs and hymns of praise relating to older religious forms have a latent healing force because they have created within the ethereal atmosphere an archetype or shape which becomes a chalice of power. So when these old songs and liturgies are sounded, they can bring peace and harmony because power is evoked within the inner planes by the use of those sound forms.

With instantaneous healing, is this a point when the healer achieves perfect meditation while they are healing?

Not only does the healer achieve this breaking through into the realm of universal life and perfection, but the patient is also momentarily uplifted above the limitations of the mind and body. Like one bird uplifted by the strength of another, they come together and are upraised momentarily in unity to this great Source of life and perfection, and through this comes the instantaneous healing.

One remembers the Master Jesus performing that healing by the laying on of hands.

Truly, but Master Jesus had the ability to love those who were sick and to feel such compassion that through his love he created a unity from himself to the sufferer. It is this unity that is needed before the healer may lift the sufferer into the realm of universal healing. Not only must he learn through meditation to come into this more perfect state of unfoldment, but he must learn to love his brother man and sister woman, not with abstract love, but to see in them the intrinsic beautiful soul that is there.

In your work of healing you often have the desire to help, but you do not know how to love each other. So go forth! Learn to overlook each others' faults, learn to encourage the weak and to uplift the fallen because of the universal love which surges within your heart.

Let your thought go forth in healing unto other creatures of the earth and let your living magnetic force radiate unto all things that you see, all things that you touch.

Remember, do not live unto yourselves alone, but live as part of the whole, As part of the whole let goodness, love and peace be your watchword.

CHAPTER EIGHT

Do Animals Survive Death?

Can you speak briefly about the evolution of the animal kingdom?

The animal spirit, even as the less evolved human spirit, is in a group consciousness, for many of those whom you regard as individual souls are really part of a group soul working up from a lesser plane of development. Even so is it with the creatures of the earth. They belong firstly to a group consciousness and then, as the whole soul breaks through into individualised facets of animal existence on earth, it is slowly increased in wisdom and power by what each animal brings back to the whole soul after its period of earthly life. Thus you see elephants of great power and intelligence. Firstly they are of a group, they roam the forest together, mate and love, and in time they come to know certain elemental forces. They will remember that the fierce striped creature is an enemy, and when the elephant dies this thought will be returned to the group consciousness. Thus, other animals will be born with the instinctive knowledge that the tiger is a fierce and unrelenting enemy against whom they must guard.

In time the elephant will come into contact with man, perhaps through injury, and man may use his healing herbs and skill upon the wounded flesh. Thus man establishes an understanding with this mighty creature so that the elephant will submit unto his will and come to know that he has skill and wisdom unknown to the elephant soul. On returning to the group soul at the end of life it will share this knowledge with the group, and when another elephant comes to earth it may not fear man but will submit more readily to his will, labouring for him, and thus it comes to understand more of mankind.

When that elephant dies its consciousness also returns to the group soul, but because it has gained a higher degree of intelligence by its contact with man, it remains an elephant who is more advanced than the whole group amongst whom it lives. Thus on returning to earth once more it will be known as one with great intelligence and individuality, and on dying and again returning to the group soul it will be recognised as an individual soul who can help to lead forward the whole group to a higher degree of consciousness. This is the way in which the animal group soul slowly advances.

As men develop spiritual power and knowledge which makes them masters and guides of other men, so do the creatures of the wild develop their own individuality and wisdom, making them leaders of their kind also and, when they die, guides of their own groups, leading them slowly into higher states of individuality.

If love is necessary for a full life, what about the animals in their wild state?

The animal in its own wild state, unloved by man, is ever conscious of its own sense of joy and unity with the great creative power of life. It will not feel the lack of man's individual love unless it has already become conscious of contact with man himself. But if the animal has felt the stir of devotion to the living master, then if unloved it suffers loneliness and as a result sometimes develops sickness.

Man's responsibility towards the animal creation is in giving them love and kindness, otherwise he should leave the living creatures to work out their own destiny in harmony with the great ebb and flow of the life forces. But where the animal becomes conscious of man's influence and its intelligence develops and love is awakened within the heart, then man accomplishes something of great importance, for he lifts through his own loving hands some part of the lesser creation. He individualises a part of the great group soul. When he himself leaves the mortal body to continue his life within the spiritual realm, he will find that the individualised animal will rise with him.

It is good, then, that love should be given to the animal creation?

If that love is attracted from the heart by animal creatures, it is good. If man or woman cannot love the person who is nearest but can give love and service unto such a creature, still if the channel of love is open, then it is good and should be increased.

The animals war with each other, but if they are unified by the love of man they will cease to war and learn the lesson of unity. There are some spirits who incarnate for the express purpose of trying to unify these warring parts of the animal creation. Through their efforts you will see the lion playing with a dog or cat.

If an animal is slightly vicious and refuses to respond to tenderness and kindness, when the time comes for it to depart this life will it leave that viciousness behind?

No, for the animal carries within its memory harshness and hurts inflicted upon it in a previous life experience. You who dwell within your gentle English land know little of the cruelty which man inflicts upon the creatures in his care. Even your doctors of medicine in their experiments bring about great suffering to helpless creatures, who are unable to wreak vengence or rebel against them.

Sometimes after a short sojourn within the grounds of happiness they return into the earthly experience to meet people of kindness. But their desire for revenge against man may make you say, "This is an intractable creature." Where you meet such an animal, give it your love, and even if it has to complete its life in this state of rebellion still, as it passes back again into the lands of happiness, it may carry a happier memory of the influence of man and may come again into a better state of incarnation.

If people become ill through wrong actions, why do domestic animals become ill?

Animals often absorb an impure magnetic force from the radiations of the people tending them and also become sick and ill because they are not taught to control their appetites. Men and women are not always wise in their tending, for even as they indulge their own bodies with sugar and excessive food, so do they allow the creatures in their care an excess of food or comfort which weakens the harmony of their bodies. Animals, too, feel very intensely the lack of love, or unjustness, of a master. This causes grief or loneliness. Therefore when you say that people become sick because of emotional upset, so also does the living creature.

*Why do animals have to kill other animals for food? They seem to have
no alternative food as does man.*

Try to view the whole realm of creation as a unity, then you will see
that every form of life is giving itself in a joyfulness of sacrifice unto the
other.
The moss feeds upon rock, the grass feeds upon moss, and animals
and birds feed upon the grass and herbage. Man himself exists by
reason of his food being obtained from the waters or the living herbage
of the earth, or from the sacrifice of creatures. Therefore animals in
their natural state accept this law of sacrifice.

*I find it difficult to love the destructive tendency found in certain
animals; when a cat catches and plays with a mouse, we know the mouse is
suffering.*

The cat and mouse. This is not a phase of life governed by the law of
love, and because the cat creation has this cruelty within itself which is
against the law of love, so many of them come under the care and
influence of men and women.
It is to eradicate by love this destructive tendency that the animal
soul incarnates within the cities of the earth. It may take centuries and
many, many times of teaching, but if the master or mistress would
project thought into the consciousness of the cat whom they love and
mentally say to it, "It is wrong; we do not like to destroy the birds and
mice," then gradually the cat will become less cruel in its approach to
forms of life weaker than itself. In time this intelligence would sink into
the whole consciousness of the cat creation. Not all animals live as they
should, and even as men and woman develop cruelty and disharmony
within themselves so have the lesser creation developed rebellion
against the law of love and harmony. You who are stronger in love
should help them to learn this law.

Can you tell us about animals in the spirit world?

First, I would speak of this law of harmony and love, for only in your
understanding of this can you begin to understand the animal creation.
Is it not true that where there is harmony there is an absence of fret

and fury, of fear and of hurt? Harmony stems from love, and where there is love there is a peaceful blending of component parts into one harmonious whole. So it is in your natural world for if you sit quietly in woodland or desert places you become conscious of a peace not found in the city. Here within the spiritual realm of Peace and Harmony this same law governs the relationship of persons unto each other, unto the place wherein they dwell and the animal life around them, as well as the relationship of one animal to another.

Any man or woman who loves and tends a living creature, no matter what their failures, no matter what their sins, this one at the time of death will find a friend and a guide. The animal reasons not, but only loves. In its lovingness it will welcome one who has fallen or sinned and lead them away from regret into the light, towards fulfilment, for this is part of the great and beautiful interblending of the life of the living creatures with the soul of human beings. All are part of one another, all are moving onwards and upwards in a beautiful forward going of evolution, transmutation and change that the whole earth itself may slowly become refined, etherealised and filled with the radiance of life and love.

In your desert and wilderness places of earth, until the lion is hungry he does not destroy the little antelope. Here in the spiritual realm hunger and thirst are known no more and the animals roam in great green silences. The lion, the jackal and the tiger live side by side with the beloved dogs and cats which man has loved during his earthly experiences. In the spiritual realm, man or woman may have as a companion a lion, or any other animal, if they have within themselves a sufficiency of love. Joyful it is to see them walking together or exploring the counterparts of the forest places.

The animal in its earthly existence has no sense of time as you understand it, except as it is governed by hunger and thirst and an awareness of the rhythms of master or mistress. Thus, in the spirit realm the animal may continue for many years without unhappiness because it has not the rhythm of hunger or thirst to make it aware of time, and timelessness makes "time" go swiftly by.

So, when you come to the end of your life's journey, you may step forth into spirit and find awaiting you the beloved horse upon which in your youth you rode across the flowing plains, or the gentle cat who cheered your heart, each aware of you although you may have been unaware of them.

Mankind slaughters animals so that thousands die every hour in an atmosphere of great terror. How is this regarded on your side?

In the spiritual realm it is regarded as a great wrong because man, by his interference with the natural laws of the animal creation, upsets the balance of nature. He breeds animals to his own desire and destroys them to his own desire, often in a spirit of greed and lust and with total disregard for the fear and feeling of the animals. But memory of the creature is a short one; many have simply lived in a herd consciousness in the care of man and are not yet indiviualised. So there is only a short remembrance of terror as they become aware of the slaughter places. As soon as their spirit is freed from the body the animal rejoins the herd and will enjoy itself within the "happy hunting grounds". But it would be better if man did not destroy the living creatures.

Is it wrong to have a pet put to sleep because it frets for the owner who has died?

Such an action, if carried out as an act of compassion, does no harm because the creature may be unhappy in its longing for its master or mistress who has passed to the spirit existence. The release from its body, if carried out painlessly, will but bring the soul of that creature into unity once more with the person who loved him. If for any reason you need to terminate the life of any creature, I would say: as you bring this into being, send forth to the soul of the animal the living influence of your loving thought and blessing, for truly that which is radiating from you will help it in its spirit existence.

How can one acquire harmony whilst being aware of the suffering of animals?

Harmony can only come into being deep within the spiritual self. Try to adjust your consciousness away from the thought of the suffering in the earth and think upon the happiness within the happy hunting places of spirit. If your spiritual vision can be opened to see, even for one moment, the beauty of the vast flowing plains in which animals disport themselves with an abandonment of complete joy, you will say even as I have done: "Their memory of fear lasts for such a little while. There is the joy and compensation of the creature."

When animals reincarnate, do they enter another animal life or do they progress to a higher form of life?

It depends upon the amount of intelligence or affection mankind has been able to stimulate within the soul of the animal. Throughout evolution the animal soul has become gradually changed out of its elemental and primal state into that which is extremely intelligent and affectionate, through man's influence upon certain types of animal. As he fondles a dog, so does he stimulate the sleeping divinity within the animal, and this animal soul will continue to live within the etheric world until such time as the spirit of that man no longer has interest in it. Then the animal will return unto the group soul from which it emerged, giving to it the sum total of its newly developed intelligence so that the whole group soul becomes of a higher order, and the new animal form which will be born into the world will be of a higher intelligence than previously.

But if the man (or woman) who first stimulated affection within the soul of this animal possesses sufficient warmth of love for this creature, he may continue to develop the creature's intelligence throughout the etheric world, so that the animal evolves a body of "feeling" in order to follow his master or mistress into higher states. If the love is strong enough between them, the animal soul may become externalised in the Land of Light to which the master or mistress has withdrawn. This is within my own personal experience, for my own horse has progressed through many states of consciousness and still remains with me when I withdraw into the Planes of Light.

CHAPTER NINE

Pathways to God

How can we recognise and absorb spiritual truths into our lives?

This is a soul faculty. When strengthened by quiet periods of meditation and prayerfulness your own spirit may begin to learn truths rather than hearing them expounded by one such as myself. All real spiritual development and unfoldment comes about within the inner spiritual consciousness, which then stimulates the mortal brain, so that each person may discover truth according to their own particular needs.

In trying to follow the spiritual pathway why do we feel so isolated?

Forward-going development is not really lonely or isolated, but takes place in periods of aloneness. As you become increasingly aware of your unity with spirits of Light and with others in your world with whom you have a harmonious kinship, your feeling of isolation will gradually dissolve into a great loving unity with the whole of the natural and spiritual worlds. So remember always that you are spirit, using your soul and body for only a short period of time. Use them well, giving thanks to the great Master Creator for the precious experience of life.

How might one attempt to redeem oneself while still on earth if one has done a terrible wrong?

You cannot redeem yourself by fruitless regret. You must try to right the balance by understanding that sin or wrong doing is an upsetting of unity, or balance. If you have brought harm to some part of the creation, you can set it to rights by trying to give a greater amount of good or helpful action to that part which has been so harmed. If you have brought suffering to a child, or allowed it to die in peril or pain, you may right the wrong by trying to bring into being healing, care and love to other unwanted child souls in your earthly world. If you have allowed some man to slip from a precipice so that he was hurt, then attempt to heal and help men who are lonely or trying to harm themselves by their wrongful action. Or if by taking more than your rightful share of properties you have deprived others, then provide homes for the lonely or poor, that they may have a certain degree of security. Thus by your action you will right the balance, bringing yourself into harmony. When you leave the mortal body you can look back, not with the searing pain of regret, but feeling you have cleared your consciousness by trying to heal the wrong.

If we can make amends in the spirit world for wrongful deeds done on earth, why is there any reason for reincarnation? Is this the law of karma?

Not all spirits come back into the earth existence. Some who do so have a great desire to render a particular service to the world, such as expressing a gift of music which may harmonise earth's conditions, or to bring a special gift of healing to overcome disease. Others may come because they are still filled with a desire for revenge or a feeling they were deprived of certain things in the earthly world which they greatly desired. The law of karma is not completely understood by earth's dwellers; it is simply a law of sowing and reaping. If you sow goodness and harmony in the mortal life you will reap it in the spirit life, but if you sow harmfulness, discord and destruction, then although you may set right some part of this in the spirit, the harm may be such that you feel impelled to return to the mortal existence to bring about a greater degree of harmony and healing.

Can you tell us about the kingdom of heaven? Is there such a place?

Indeed there is, but we in spirit speak of it as the realm of peace, the realm of unity and love. As the soul progresses from plane to plane in the high places of spirit it emits its own inward note of power, drawing unto itself other souls who are in harmony. While they are bonded together in this state of sympathy, love and unity are established amongst them and we say: Here is a manifestation of the kingdom of heavenly peace. Groups of such spirits may number seven, seventy times seven or beyond, but where this unity and love exist there is a beautiful harmony of colour flowing between them in rainbow formations. Through these will flash from soul to soul streaks of brilliant light, the symbol of their sympathetic thought. Such unity and love creates beautiful blossoms in all the surrounding atmosphere, the air becomes clear and bright, and because harmony brings forth sound, music is evoked from the deep bell-like note emanating from the inward consciousness of each soul within the group. This is our understanding of the heavenly state.

What about Christians, those who loved and served Jesus so willingly? Is there no place where they can be with him?

There is such a place, the equivalent of the heaven created by the myriad men and women who have visualised this land of gleaming light in which white-robed throngs move with joy and in which the lovers of the Master Jesus dwell within his kingdom. This is known as the great realm of Christly love, where many of your people come when they end their earthly life experience, but not all who have been baptised into Christianity or who call themselves Christians, only those who have deeply and unflinchingly loved the Master Jesus. Throughout the centuries there are those in religious communities who devoted their lives in love unto him, those who nursed and sacrificed themselves in service for love of him. All these, receiving the blessing that flows from his heart may be rededicated to service and may come into your midst bearing his imprint upon themselves so that you sometimes say, "These are Christ-like souls," and may even think it is the Christ himself.

The state of spirit experience known to you as the Summerland, the land of eternal peace and beauty, this too is a kind of heaven, a place to which gentle and kindly people come, those who have no deep inward religious convictions, but who have led lives of simple goodness and harmony.

You speak of the Christ plane, or the plane of Christly love. Is it the highest plane in the spirit world?

It is the highest plane which you who dwell in this land can understand because to you the aspect of the Christ is indeed the purest and highest one, but there are other planes of spirit influence which are equally beloved and high to which persons of other religious thought go. There is also another state beyond, but it is impossible to bring this into the comprehension of the mortal mind.

It has also been said that the kingdom of heaven is within. What does that mean?

Apart from its reality in the spirit world it is a state of consciousness, for you may find your kingdom whilst still in the mortal body. When you are with those you love and peace lies upon your soul like a silvery mantle, then indeed you are finding a small reflection of the greater kingdoms of peace in the life of the spirit. If you train yourselves to live lovingly with those around you, you gain such a heightened and purified state of understanding that you can come into attunement with the higher state of the kingdom of heaven and tune your heart to the Christly realm. Those you love greatly, the beloveds of your heart, your departed brothers, husbands or wives, while you tune your love to them: you may sometimes reach out to the Summerland wherein they dwell, or by raising your consciousness in the quietude of meditation you can find unity with the spirit group of your own particular affinity, through which waves of peace, music and colour may vibrate unto you whilst you are still on the earth.

How do we know that what we believe is truth? Should we try to convince others when we feel we have that truth?

The truth can only be truth to each man and woman according to their inner understanding. You should remember this. Because you find a certain truth is good or a certain pathway is right, you should not endeavour to force your brother or sister to go that way. The wise man and woman, the seeker after truth, says to others on the way: "I have seen this, I have heard this. This I have experienced." If what is said vibrates an answering chord within the consciousness of the other, then that one may desire to learn from you, but not all have the same thought. It is right for some to learn through the way of love, some through the way of simplicity or sacrifice, yet for others the way lies through beauty or service. For each soul there is an individual way which is right. It is for you to guide the steps of your seeking, groping brothers and sisters into the way which is right for *them*.

But remember: unto the child must be given toys and a simple teaching, unto the wise man a thought which is pure and lofty. For some the way is in silence. Each of you, garnering knowledge and experience, may share what you have.

The law of life and the law of the spirit is that there is continuous creation and re-creation. There is no stagnation. Therefore you must give and you must receive, pouring out that which you have so that an inner replenishment may come. You may not stand still nor keep your wisdom or your healing to yourself, for to do so is contrary to the law of the Master Creator.

There are many beliefs and philosophies, yet all think their way is best?

When you come to the end of your earthly experience and step forth from the physical body into the new life it will not be asked of you: "What religion did you follow? What belief did you hold?" There will be none to say: "Were you a Roman Catholic, a Hindu, a Jew or a Christian?" But those who have loved you in your earth life, these will come to you with love. They will look to see how much service you have rendered, how much love you have given to those weaker and less evolved than yourself, how much courage you have shown in dark and lonely experiences, for by this measure is the soul known when it comes to the spirit life. But where spiritual knowledge has given the soul increased ability to live kindly and peacefully, then we say that religious belief has its value. Where a philosophy helps to raise the thoughts on high, then that philosophy is a true one. But it is not true that worship in any one church or belief or any one religion is more important than the other?

Why is it considered necessary by certain religions to make blood sacrifices?

It is so because man in earlier states of progress and knowledge regarded the blood as something so potent, so wonderful and so mysterious that to him it represented the very essence of the being.

In past centuries man was not able to peer into the body, to open it and see the marvels of circulation. His only knowledge came when the body was wounded or cut, and he then discovered that what appeared to be brown had become red, and what appeared to be black in the surface texture of the skin was stained by the wonderful ruby red flow which came from within. In the simplicity of his thought the blood seemed a most potent and mystic force. He worshipped it because he thought that blood was the actual life, and therefore the most wonderful offering he could give unto the Unknown. It is this mystic aspect of the letting of blood which comes through into your own world today, and is still embodied in the most beautiful symbolism which was given by the Master Jesus when he tried to take man's mind from the thought of blood unto the symbolism of the wine.

As you move forward into a more subtle understanding, with the knowledge we are trying to release, men and women are coming to see that the soul, the spirit, is the living individual: it is apart from the blood and the wine. So men and women are learning to offer themselves, their thoughts, their own personal magnetism, offering it in service and worship as they give themselves to healing and to the blessing of earth's creation.

We are hoping that in the passage of years people will meet in temples or churches with the simpler offering of holding forth their hands as the most mystic part of their spiritual ritual, that from their hands the magnetic force will flow, creating a living circuit that may become the emblem of healing and of renewal.

Your healing circles will become more highly developed and will form the most mystic ritual in the services of an age which is still coming into being. Even as the blessing of wine only becomes truly sanctified by the magnetic force given through the fingers of the priest, even so the hands of your healers bless, and the searchers of truth may come to receive a true spiritual baptism transmitted from on high through the prepared vessels.

How can the perfect God also be the God of evil?

One of the aspects of the great Creative Spirit is to be found in creativeness or reconstruction, which means that if this is so there must also be destruction. So the power of the Master Creator is indeed in the destructive forces at work within His universe, but we would not call these forces "evil". The only evil we recognise is the evil force which man has set into motion within his own world, which is the desecration of his own knowledge of good. But even there the Master Creator cannot be separated from His own creation. As man is invested with a will of his own, I do not think it is either wise or good to ascribe unto the Maker of man the errors which man himself has perpetrated in his endeavour to learn how to use his creative power.

How far can we believe the Bible sayings of Jesus? Is he the greatest of the teachers?

The Master Jesus is not necessarily the greatest of the teachers, for all come with a message which is for the people of their time. The teachings of love which he gave have indeed been recorded and kept in a high degree of purity. Had those teachings been adhered to by the people who claim to be Christians, then indeed a great cleansing of the errors of man's fault—which we call evil—would have taken place. The teachings of Jesus are correct because they are the teachings of love, and for the people of his time he was indeed the greatest teacher.

Have you, or anyone you have met, seen God?

Not in the sense in which you speak of God. I have seen the glory, and I think it is the glory which is known to the people of earth as God.

Before I decided to come back to labour amongst the people on earth, from the gateway of the seventh sphere I looked forth and beheld the glory of the spirit—the heart of Light—for such you will call it. I think it is this which has become known as God to the peoples of earth, who have captured this word from the singers in the ancient scriptures who spoke of the glory of God.

It is not possible to describe in ordinary language the radiance and beauty of His power, but if you can visualise some mighty lake lying calm, translucent and unmoving, and then gleaming upon it the radiance of a sun which is soft, beautiful as moonlight and yet without the vagueness of moonlight; and within the heart of this radiance a centre like a glowing heart, rosy, gentle, palpitating and throbbing throughout the whole, and then try to feel that this enormous stillness, a

radiance palpitating with life and love was flowing in and through you
and through all things . . . then you might have some vague symbol of
understanding of that which we know as the Glory.

*I know someone who claims to have seen Jesus. Is this possible, or was it
some other high spirit?*

Even as the beloveds who love each other in the earthly realm gather
a likeness one unto the other because they faithfully seek to portray the
qualities which they see within the beloved one, even so is it within the
great Christ sphere of light. Those who love the Master with a mighty
love can, after a time, take on his likeness and give forth a radiance like
unto his radiance, so that some passing by will say: "Truly, is this not
the Nazarene? Is this not the Master himself?" Who can divide the
beloved from the lover? Who can say wherein the separation arises?
None shall say, for within this mighty Christ realm of love there is such
unity, such power, such beauty, that many who go forth to serve,
drawing near to those who love the Nazarene in the earthly realm,
because of their close likeness unto him will cause the earthly one to
say, "Here indeed has been the Master in our midst."

So, I think the one of whom you speak saw a serving spirit in the
Master's group who, coming into earthly conditions, carries so strong
an impress of the Master's love that he seems to the looker to be in the
form of Jesus himself.

*Sometimes it seems we are in a position similar to that of Jesus in our
efforts to give forth a teaching which is different to the orthodoxy of our
time. We meet with much misunderstanding and hurt.*

This is partly true, for all that happens to the individual has been
symbolised in the New Testament as that which happened to the
Master Jesus. Therefore when you stand as a teacher of that which you
have seen as true, laying before your neighbour your revelation, then in
a small measure you outpicture through your own life many of the
experiences through which Jesus himself passed.

There will be times when all seem to misunderstand your meaning,
times when you feel you are being crucified by the hands or words of
others, through your time of little death when your dearest hopes or

treasured desires have to be laid aside, as in the coldness of the tomb. In this you will be outpicturing some part of the Christly teaching. Then you will rise in new strength, confirmed in the power of your truth, aware of the influence of the angelic beings guiding you, and standing upon the pinnacle of your own experience from you light will stream forth, as it streamed forth upon the Easter morning.

As you evolve, so you become an enchristed soul yourself, revealing in your fashion that which will illumine and heal some part of the soul of the world immediately surrounding you. Therefore, be strong! As you grow in knowledge eventually you become like miniature Christs, lifting upon your shoulders some part of the woe of the world itself, and suffering the taunts of the ignorant, slowly you transform it through your own love into purified understanding, which becomes wisdom. So, outward through you there streams the revelation of the spirit.

Regarding the death of Christ. Was that ordained?

It was not ordained, but Jesus involved himself in certain conditions of the earthly world; he fought the power of the priests and Romans, and therefore precipitated the crisis which culminated in his death, but he could have acted differently. He could have refused to go down to Jerusalem. Had he refused then he would not have been crucified.

Which would have been the better way, to have gone or to have refused?

I think it would have been better had he refused. A lot of people would not, agree because they have grown into the understanding that through this death something more wonderful came to the world. But I think something just as wonderful would have grown in the world had he lived longer in the midst of his people.

The Bible describes the Master Jesus as "a man of sorrows and acquainted with grief". Can you comment upon this?

That is a wrong description; those who were the writers of these manuscripts thought only of his suffering and of the pain he endured. They forgot that in himself he had a joy which attracted the children who loved to follow in his footseps, as well as the simple men who, not being wise in the ways of wisdom, nevertheless could recognise goodness in another being. Would those simple fishermen of the earth have felt happy and at peace with a man who never smiled? Would they not rather feel oppressed by a man acquainted only with sorrow and grief? The Master Jesus, just as all others, feeling the great upliftment and power of the spirit, knew such joy that he could convey it unto those surrounding him.

It is said that Jesus went to other teachers or sources of wisdom to study and obtain knowledge; is this so?

This is true, for Jesus the man is distinct from the spirit who overshadowed him. Even as you, a potential medium may go to see the works of other mediums and may learn in your own self, as distinct from the spirit who may overshadow you, even so did he. Is it not recorded that the voice came, the spirit overshadowed and descended upon him and spoke, saying, "This is my beloved child"?

Jesus the teacher remains very close to this your earthly world, and in his influence may often project to those who love him some thought or expression of his own personality. It is quite true and possible that if you love this Master then he will direct to you his blessing and thought.

Was the Christ spirit in Jesus when he was born?

The boy Jesus was not overshadowed by the great spirit of the Christ until he reached the time of his baptism, when it was seen by those watching as something like the spirit of a beautiful bird descending from the heavens, for always the human eye must interpret that which it sees in the symoblism of the earthly world. But as this spirit spoke, saying, "This is my beloved son," Jesus and the Christ had indeed become one, as mediums become one with the overshadowing spirit who may teach or heal through them. In becoming ensouled by this great spirit of Divine love, the beautiful power of Christly love entered into Jesus and spread out all around and about him, so that the earth itself became interpenetrated by the love aspect of the Master Creator.

When the life of Jesus the Master ceased, the Christly influence continued, as even now in your world today it still continues in beauty and power.

What did Jesus mean when he said to those whom he was teaching "I come not to bring peace but a sword"?

The Master Jesus gave unto his beloved ones the secret of the peace of the spirit symbolised as a sword, the sword of truth. But it is also a symbol of balance. A swordsman must first learn how to balance body, hand and brain so that he may quickly and safely use his sword, else his sword will destroy him. So, all who learn to use the sword, be it the weapon of defence or the spiritual symbol of the sword itself, equally they must learn balance. Until you have balance in the mind and the emotions, until you learn to use your eyes to discern truth and know truth in the world about you, how may you use the sword of truth harmoniously and well? Unless you are balanced within yourself you will destroy, maim and harm the spiritual souls of the people around you.

But where is the point of balance? Where is the centre of rhythm and poise? It lies within the inward consciousness, in the central place of your own soul and spirit. So you must, each one, learn to find this and come back again and again unto this deep centre. For if in the midst of battle and destruction you know deep within your heart that all this is but the outward show and within yourself you are at peace, then all this activity will not destroy you or bring you harm, for this centre within the heart is of the spirit, and the power of the spirit can overcome all the restlessness and destructiveness of the earthly conditions.

But it may often seem to you, immersed in this world of action, that the swirling movement or unrest is the reality, until such time that you gain your moment of spiritual understanding and see that the true reality is the power of the spirit.

What is the true meaning of prayer?

The spirit coming into earthly life becomes self-centred, for it is at the very centre of the being that it has created. But if the incarnating spirit is to return to the remembrance of its own spiritual state it must break out of its self-centred concern, and it is in this that the value of prayerfulness is to be understood.

True prayer consists in reaching out from within unto something, a power, a person, an ideal. Thus a straight ray is thrust forth, so that as you pray you are creating the first living emblem of your desire to escape from the globe of etheric substance surrounding you.

The child breathes forth some simply worded prayer, laying the first step by which it will later rise out of its inner concern with self, outward into a comprehension of the mighty powers surrounding it. The habit is established before the personality becomes too strongly formed within the inner soul and before the etheric substance surrounding the spirit has become an encasement hardened by years of experience. You sometimes say a person has become encased in a shell of selfishness. This shell is the hardening of the outer circumference of the spiritual aura, the protective etheric body in which the spirit itself is hidden.

We cannot easily reach people on earth who are thus contained within this shell of their inward self-concern, until sorrow has evoked the desire for prayer. When prayer streams forth from the anguished spirit, then straight rays of endeavour and clear flames of prayerful thought emerge and the encircling activity in the aura is stilled. Then through the entries so created we pour in our spiritual comfort and wisdom, our desire to heal and free the beloved whom we have been longing to help.

So, try to see your life and unfoldment as something dependent upon the steps of prayer. The simple prayer of childhood giving way to the surging prayer of the heart when in youth you pray for the person you love and things you desire to attain. For if in praying for things for yourself your prayer is later concerned in gaining these things that they may enrich the life of another, then it becomes a stepping stone unto true prayer, which is the forgetting of self in the remembrance of the needs of others. Later in life, when sickness occurs or death takes those who are beloved, still do you add further steps of prayer, in endeavouring to discover unity with the great Central Source of Power.

Prayer truly expressed becomes a living quality which impregnates the chair upon which you sit, the articles you use and the very clothes you wear, for streaming out from the inner soul it is the living force of the spirit itself.

Are prayers wasted when directed to selfish or unresponsive people?

It may not be immediately received by them, but there is a law of the spirit which we call the "law of accumulative power or wisdom." Thus, if prayer is sent forth for a soul who is closed to reception of its influence, nevertheless this thought force will accumulate within the spiritual ether until such time as it may find its way through, bringing blessing and light. Meanwhile, the one who has loved and prayed is enriched because givingness always enlarges the consciousness of the giver.

What is the best way to pray?

I would say to you that you may deliver the message unto others, "Pray often and love much, for in prayer and in loving shall lie your strength."

Often it is said, "We pray frequently and our lives are dedicated unto prayer," but where there is no love then there is no prayer. Those who love much pray often, for the life of love becomes a symbol of the life of prayer. Prayer truly is the shedding forth into the spiritual life the desires and searchings of the individual. Where there is much love then indeed is there a searching and a seeking into all the surrounding atmosphere for that which may be best for the beloved, and not only best for the one beloved, but for all those who are the beloveds of the heart.

Therefore, love greatly, love frequently and love widely. Accept in your loving the hurts which may come to you through that lovingness, for these hurts truly are but the spurs which lead you on to greater prayer. Where the beloved brings unto you disappointment or hurt, then is there not the striving in the inward soul towards greater understanding and a deeper perception? This striving itself is the very essence of prayer. Where there is prayer and love within the human heart, then is there lit in the centre of the being a pure flame which spreads and glows and sheds its glory far and wide around you.

Make of your lives the simple effort towards a greater lovingness and think not, "I should pause now to say my words of prayer," but rather say as you handle the substances of the earth and prepare work to be used by those whom you love, "This indeed is the symbol of my prayer in that my hands have served." When you look with the eye of affection and compassion upon those who come seeking for help, then you may say, "This truly is a prayer," for where there is love within the heart so also is that love expressed in the prayer of blessing which is the benediction given through the glance of your eye. As you grow in love, so do you also grow in prayerfulness.

So simple is the way and so clear the key to understanding that it is for you, even in this time and place, to lift up your eyes and see how clear is the way before you, and yet in the multiplicity of the human life so soon do you fall from this understanding of truth, so soon become lost in the mazes of difficult thought.

Inscribe upon your hearts and memories these simple words: "To love often is to pray much, and to pray much in the true essence of prayer is to love very greatly," and where love and prayer dwell together, then is the peace added unto peace, light added unto light, experience deepening other experience, until the soul indeed enters into the comprehension of its God.

Is it better to pray as an individual or with a group?

It is better to pray in your own individual and interior fashion, for these outward forms of prayer have come into being amongst organised religions of the world that the poor, the lost and the ignorant may always have some aid by which they can be drawn into a higher state of consciousness. The souls who are growing in knowledge, increasing in their own interior state of self-consciousness, these should come into the spirit through the quietude of interior meditation and prayer, for eventually the true way to unfoldment must be the individual pathway of the soul, and each one walks the way alone. It is only in the first stages of progress that community worship and community prayer is a help unto the soul. The further the soul advances, the more individual the way has to become.

If we do not forgive a person who injures us do we also darken and injure the soul of that person?

If you send forth hatefulness and bitterness toward that other one and they are sensitive to your influence they will certainly absorb some of the negative emanation you send forth. Forgiveness and understanding is of tremendous importance, not just for the small personal hurts, but to forgive the wounds which the soul of the world experiences when great numbers of people die in fire, in water, in famine, explosion or war. The death and suffering of large groups of people makes a stain on the world soul because of the bitterness felt by their children, parents or friends. When you repeat your prayer and say, "Forgive us as we forgive them," remember that you are asking to make forgiveness for the community, for the world, and you ask that others may similarly learn to forgive. The pattern of your prayer is beautiful, so pray with understanding from the heart, giving forth love and forgiveness in every possible way.

In the Bible it says "In the beginning was the Word". What is the word?

The word is the causative sound. In the first stages of creation and in the higher regions of spirit existence all things resolve into sound or vibration; this is sometimes perceived as colour. It is from this vibrating sound that the atoms of your mortal world are set into motion and maintained in their particular patterns. These appear as trees, houses or human beings. When you seek for an understanding of the primal essence and the first great cause, then you discover there is Sound, known as the Word, for surely the Word and Sound are similar.

Is sound applicable as a creative force in revival meetings where there is a lot of singing? Are the war cries of primitive people similar?

Sound is created not only in the inner being of the ones who sing and cry forth but there is also an evocation of the power or energy which has been stored in the spiritual realm by those who have used that sound in preceding times. So when you sing or speak the Lord's Prayer, this invariably brings to the singer an energy, a blessing, for the sounding of the words evokes within the inner planes a response which brings to the sayer a prayer protection, an increase of spiritual force.

In spirit I sometimes see the storage place of this sound of the Lord's Prayer like a twisted lily shape of light containing the crystallised sound vibration from the many people who have sounded the prayer throughout centuries of earthly time. Around this are guardian spirits who regard it as their holy prayer: Christian spirits who lived as nuns or monks, giving to it new energy and fresh light from their own being, that this prayer shape may still give to earth's pray-ers the blessing and power they need.

Is there a Hell as described in Christian religion, a place of fire and torment?

Yes there is. It has been created by the thoughts of men and women through centuries of earth time. They have visualised this place, creating a condition so fraught with fear that unenlightened spirits, not yet freed from their selfish desires people, it and may torment any who come within the radius of this realm, which is beyond the confines of the earth.

But it is not created by the Power of all Good for the punishment of the errors of souls on earth. Those who enter this place are drawn only by their guilty desires or by the weight of their own inward state of selfishness. If within themselves they have the shining light of true love then they rapidly find their way out into truer planes of spiritual experience. So, do not fear "Hell". Do not fear punishment. Do not contribute to it any power of your thoughts, thus building it into a stronger pattern, but light the candles of faith and truth that such a place may slowly dissolve and fade from the consciousness of humankind and from the astral atmosphere near your earth.

This place *is* slowly beginning to fade, but it still has its existence, just as the heaven visualised by people for hundreds of years, the heaven paved with gold, having structures gleaming with jewels. It is not a real place of spirit existence but a little heaven built by orthodox thoughts of those who subscribe to it.

Sometimes if we can help a soul in no other way we take them to this little heaven, that walking therein for a while they feel, "Yes, this is what I expected." Then, as they grow tired of it, we may lead them on into other ways of useful service and further progression.

The power of thought is of tremendous creative intensity: it has the power of the creative energy of God acting through the mind of the living soul of man. Therefore, learn to use your thought rightfully, hopefully, truthfully and lovingly, that you may create for those whom you love on earth their own little heaven, and in all the world about you light, peace and beauty, for these are the conditions you will later inherit when you leave your mortal body and pass into the higher heritages of spiritual experience.

Will God allow man to destroy the world by nuclear bombs? Will He allow misuse of this knowledge to cause countless malformed babies to be born to future generations?

This world, which you think so permanent, is but part of the worlds which have existed throughout long centuries of time, in which nations have risen and fallen, cities have been built and destroyed, forms of animal life have risen, taken their experience and have been transmuted into other forms of life. In this evolution, races of men and women have come, reached the final evolvement of their understanding, then they too have gone on to other worlds of experience.

Why then should you fear? Why be so dismayed at the thought of some mighty change or cataclysm in this part of your mortal experience? The earth is old and has endured light and darkness, heat and cold; it has borne upon its bosom many forms of life. It has seen the rising of great joys, the tears of great sorrow, and yet the body of the earth endures, for it is a place of experience, the planet of sacrifice, the planet of purification.

Shall this cease because one or two men in their search for understanding learn how to change the atomic structure? Surely such a thought is of the mind only and not of the spirit! The earth will endure until it is no longer a useful school for spirits needing purification, needing to learn the lessons of sacrifice. The earth will endure until the ethers have been cleansed, changed and bathed in the love of men and women, until the Master Creator no longer has use for the earthly planet within His great worlds of creative life.

Therefore lift up your hearts from the darkened valley of fear, lift your consciousness into the great rivers of life and say, "All is well, all must be well, for we are part of a greater universe than ever we can see or know while we are bonded by mortal mind and mortal thought."

Can you define spirituality?

Spirituality is when the spiritual mind is dominant and overcomes the many activities and desires of the mortal mind, which are to be found in greed, acquisitiveness, restlessness, or the effort of gaining many things not always needful to the health or harmony of the body. When the mundane mind becomes blended with the spiritual mind, then many of these mortal attributes are dissolved, and the mundane mind will be used to accomplish work, to explain or be used in a concrete fashion for the work entailed, but it will not be the dominant mind just desiring or fulfilling its own pleasures, rather it is working at the direction of the spiritual consciousness.

In dying, did Jesus take away the sins of the world?

This belief and teaching that the Master Jesu died to redeem the world has within itself a deep and profound truth. He did not die to take upon himself the sins of the people, but in his dying and bearing of pain and ignorance he was able to transmute and transform them, setting into motion streams of healing, light and truth by which earth's ignorance became transformed and earth's sickness became healed and purified. In this way redemption took place even as it is taking place now in your world through the myriads of enchristed souls who are slowly giving themselves in love and service to redeem the earth from its errors, darkness and pain.

So be strong! Be strong in your moments of temptation and despair, remembering that when all seems dark this may be the moment when, by the death of your little self, the resurrection of the new enchristed self may come into being.

Is there judgement after death?

There is the soul's own judgement of itself, and often the most difficult moment for the soul is when it is divested of the pretences with which it covered itself in earthly life. We do not look upon the new-born souls with judgement: we look upon them with love. If into your midst now there came a child from the street, dirty and dishevelled, and when its garments were removed and the child stood before you naked you saw upon its body the soil which needed washing away, and the scars gained in battling with adverse conditions, you would not look with judgement but with pity, love and tenderness.

Even so do those in the Places of Light look upon the soul newly come, for we have walked the way of the earthly experience, we had our failures, our times of stress and difficulty, and most of us bear upon our soul some scar of that suffering. How then should we judge the other beloveds when they come? Looking upon them we remember our own struggles and therefore we look upon them with love.

This is how it should be in your ways of earthly life. Instead of looking upon each other in self-righteous judgement you should, by the depths of your love and understanding, reach out your hand to strengthen the weak and to encourage each other in times of despondency, so that slowly and surely you may come into fellowship and unity of soul.

Does the festival of Christmas have any spiritual effect? Does it have influence upon the spirit plane?

Prior to the coming of your Christmas time there is a great stirring and activity within the summerlands of joy. Parents and loved ones of those still incarnate within the body come close to the earth, imparting unto them rays of their happy thought. You will find that even those who have said they will take no part in Christmas finally become caught up in the great network of joyous friendship and happy giving. As this network of goodwill grows and brightens, showing here and there the bright stars of children's joy, so part of the dark pall of man's fear is lightened and the spirit ones come near to interblend their loving influence with the hearts and minds of all those they have loved as they gather in silent unity with family groups. Then light shafts of prayer begin to arise as hearts are opened unto the Christ Centre, that the blessing of the Christ may be received within the earth.

Those who are the guardians, the guides, the watching angels, withdraw from the earth for a time, returning unto their rightful realms of light, there to hold their own festival by being reunited with kindred spirits, those they left when they undertook work for humanity within the mortal plane. These groups turn their attention upward unto the great Centre of light and peace, for at this season the Christ remembers again the world in which He once took his earthly journey. A mighty shaft of light, a great outpouring of love is sent forth to be received firstly by the guardian ones who have withdrawn for a time from their earthly labours, and then to those who wait upon the next planes, so that it becomes a mighty silver shower of light dripping from the fingers of one unto the other, dripping in rays of light from them unto others, flowing on and on until it comes to the happy family spirits who are united with those at the fireside places, that part of the Christmas joy and love may come to them too.

Unto those who prepared their hearts in quietness of prayer and meditation, their attention turned upwards unto the Centre of light, unto them Christly blessing comes clear and pure, not diluted or transmitted by family souls, but as a precious silvery dew taken into their hearts and shed out again in peace and holiness. With this great release of light and power a great cleansing takes place, causing all within the high places to sing together great hymns of joy. Those in the mortal body find themselves lifting up their voices in praise, joining in the hymns once known unto the parents and grandparents of old.

Indeed it is a glorious festival, but man sometimes forgets to receive the beauty of the Christly power and thinks only that he may eat and drink. But you who are growing in knowledge may tune your heart to the Heart of Love to receive the Christly blessing.

Apart from the star of Bethlehem, was there any other indication of the birth of Jesus?

It was known unto the seers of that time that a boy would enter into earthly existence to undertake a special work. So when the infant child was brought to the temple, the old woman possessing the gift of seership could see by the spiritual light in this child's aura that here was an incarnation of a beautiful spirit, one who had a great spiritual destiny. She was also able to see those bright and shining guides or guardians who companioned him during the years of his earthly growth. Therefore, as she took the infant into her arms, so in a measure was she like the mediums of your own time, who rejoice when on holding a child thus, they are aware of the spiritual destiny of the little one.

Is there a deeper meaning to the Christmas story?

The essential truths of the soul and spirit are so simple that a child can understand them, yet because they are so simple men and women run hither and thither seeking for a deeper meaning, something which can be clothed in the cleverness of the earth language.

Come back from the complicated study and enter into the beauty of this season with the simplicity of the child, for love and nobility were born into the world in the symbolism of the Christly child just as they are each time an infant lies within its mother's arms. Look upon the beauty of this symbol with eyes which see clearly the tremendous power of its spiritual truth, and think upon that which is pure, holy and beautiful, for the laws of the Master Creator are not complicated. They are the simple laws of sowing and reaping, of change and transmutation, of life and death, inbreathing and outbreathing. Hold fast to the beauty and simplicity of these rhythms and meditate upon the rise and fall of the life force manifesting in the changing seasons, and in the coming and going of the sun. These are as simple as the law of love, the truth that love endures and can transcend the many miles which may separate those upon earth, even as it transcends the separation which arises between life and death. These are the fundamental truths of your life and world: why complicate them? Divest yourselves of the garments of learning, lay upon one side the shields whereby you defend yourselves against the arguments of the outer world, and think upon that which is too simple for the comprehension of the ordinary mind and can only be understood by the soul itself in the purity of meditation and prayer.

So, at this Christmas season reflect upon the beauty of love symbolised in the simplicity of the new born child bringing hope, peace and power unto all.

If some of the Roman Catholic church teachings are in error, do Catholics find trouble with this when they die?

Only partly, for inward truth is there to be discerned by a sufficiently sensitive soul. When they pass to spirit others who have preceded them, sisters, priests, enlightened Christians, will be there to meet them and bring the wider understanding they need. But some who enter holy orders simply fulfil the rituals without light, living in bitterness and unenlightenment. Such nuns, monks or priests leave the mortal body encased in their own aura of darkness, unaware of the power of the lighter spirits, and such remain in the lower atmosphere interpenetrating the earth.

In spirit, is the Master Jesus in a human form?

He projects his image into the imagery of human form, but in himself he is pure light, to be seen as pure light by those who seek to perceive him. If he desired to send a special message to one in the mortal body, he would project his blessing into one of the Jesus souls close to him in his own heaven, and that one would convey the blessing and might be seen as a Jesus spirit, but holding his own particular form. It could be likened to a degree of entrancement when a high spirit entrances one of a slightly lesser order, enabling them to penetrate into the heavier atmosphere surrounding the mortal world. So Jesus may not come directly in his own spiritual form of radiant light, but through one of his messengers.

Can you explain the meaning of the remark made by Jesus at the Last Supper, when he said to his disciples, "This is my body, this is my blood"?

I think he was but trying to symbolise that the body is composed of the matter of the earth. Even as the bread, the wheat, draws it life from the earth and is of the earth, earthy, so is the body of a similar nature. The wine is the fluid of the earth, the juice within the grape.

What happens when a whole nation prays, for instance in time of war?

The united prayer of a great body of people praying together in sincerity and purity of intent creates a mighty ray of light which rises through the near earth world upwards through the spheres of spirit experience until it reaches the Centre of Power itself. But if the prayer is tainted with the desire for acquisition, if the nation prays for victory that they may have domination over other peoples, then it does not so rise. Similarly, when it is shrouded in fear. But if the prayer is breathed forth from the agony of the human heart, winged with the protective love of mothers for their children, desiring spiritual help that the helpless may be succoured and the little ones protected, then indeed it rises in the purity of its light. As with nations so with groups, churches and circles. A prayer winged with earnest desire for the blessing of the whole rises to great heights and brings back great answers.

Sometimes a person who never normally prays will do so when confronted with sudden dramatic circumstances, and their prayer seems to be swiftly answered. Why is this?

Can you not see that such a one, having little understanding of spiritual things, must be encouraged to see proof of this power? Therefore when their prayer is breathed forth, the mother, husband or loving friend who is near within the spirit life will swiftly bring an answer to their prayer, that the flame of faith may be lighted to glow with new fervour, and their spiritual progression hastened by their belief in the action of prayer.

But when you have steadfastly prayed for progress and spiritual growth with sincere desire from the depths of your soul, then carelessly sometimes you pray for things you desire as a child desires toys, then the answer may not be vouchsafed, for you are not children. In this way you will learn to wait patiently, bowing to the wisdom of wills stronger and higher than yours. But the prayer is taken, regarded, and kept in safe keeping by those who watch over you, and in good time the answer may be given and the power shown. Remember, it is the sincerity of your desire and the purity of your intent that gives your prayer wings.

Man often says, "God has answered my prayer," but if he had the open eye of vision he would see a loved one standing near watching over the progress of this soul who says, "Here is a sincere desire which we will try to bring to fruition that the spiritual progression may be forwarded."

What was the special revelation given by Jesus when he grew to manhood?

He revealed the great love aspect of the Master Creator which became symbolised as the Christly spirit. Jesus was indeed a fine and beautiful vessel through whom the revelation of the Christ could be given unto the earthly world, especially in the need of that time when the harshness of the religious rulers had stolen joy from the hearts of the people. The Christ is the ensoulment of love, and through whom all healing, tenderness and beauty can be understood by earth's children.

Of what nature is God and how may we grow toward Him?

Firstly, you need new understanding of the relationship between yourselves and the great Creator of the universe. The old idea that God the father is in some distant place in the heavens to be approached with awe and trembling must be supplanted by the inner teaching of unity; that man's soul should be in unity with the power of the Creator manifesting through all things.

The teachers of the past taught that your world is complete in itself. That is untrue. It is but part of a chain of worlds and stars strung out through all the vast spaces of the universe, each having its effect upon the other as are beads each one part of a string of pearls, with the string binding them together itself but part of the whole. The old thought that man is bound to the life of the world and that your God is concerned only with this little bead should be replaced with a purer comprehension of the power and majesty of the Creator who holds within his left hand the worlds which are revolving in shadow and in his right hand those revolving in brilliant light. The Creator who sets into motion the great laws of balance, one force balancing another, that all is kept harmoniously in a slow, beautiful ordered progression. Through this moving and balancing, the souls and spirits of the living creatures also take their ways from life to life and from star to star. As the string moves within the beads threaded upon it, so does the great life of the Creator move through all created things.

Secondly, you must define how you yourselves symbolise God, and into what form and shape you desire to grow. Here in the spirit life our vision of God is this great creative love energy moving in and through all things. If you desire to grow towards this God, this great Master Creator, then indeed you must learn to look to the power and glory manifesting through all the creative world surrounding you. Look through the windows of your soul, feel with the fingers of your soul and listen with the ears of your soul and know the glory of your God.

Take into your hands a raindrop as it glistens upon the bough and see with your inward soul that in this drop of water is all colour. Let your soul become conscious of the creative power of the Master Spirit who makes colour, then ask yourself by what creative effort has this drop of water been distilled from the sky, from that you can behold its visible nature upon your hand? As you understand the raindrop, so do you grow toward God. Then lift a tiny petal from the smallest blossom and behold the miracle of gleaming colour, its texture, shape and perfume. As you think upon it, grow toward God in remembrance that this is but one of a myriad unseen petals in untold splendour of beauty upon the lonely mountainsides and in the farmost places. Stretch your soul, growing away from your own immediate concern into the larger consideration of the works of God.

Cease for a while the whirling thoughts that are concerned with your own life and look upon another human being, the one nearest to you. See the miracle of flesh and bone, the lines carved upon the face by laughter or sorrow, see the fire of anger, the softness of love. Look not with indifference but see them as the temple of the living God and let your soul stretch and grow. Feel with the soul's sensitive fingers the agony and joy which has taken place within this man or woman, then let your thought flow on and on to others of a like nature, to the aged and the young, the helpless and the able, those in far and near lands. So shall your soul stretch and grow, the tendrils of your awareness reaching out and out, growing toward nature, humanity, and toward God.

Here in the spirit places we have to learn in this way. We gain no wisdom or expansion without effort, but only by growing in understanding the one of the other. Even so must you upon earth, for by loving the created and understanding the created, so can you grow toward the glory and the life of the Creator.

We are told that some spirits are in purgatory while others are said to be earthbound. What does that mean?

They are somewhat similar states. Purgatory, as it is called by some Christian churches, is really a self-examination of the soul, a review of its opportunities while on earth and its failures. Often the soul mourns and feels remorse. It inwardly burns in sorrow, for the person is facing himself. At last a desire to work comes and it is then he sees the helpers, in the robes of light. Earthbound spirits are those who after death do not at first understand what has happened to them and think they are still within the earth life. They do not feel regret at their actions like the others mentioned, but rather a desire for the earth-life to continue. The helpers cannot reach them while they remain in this state.

Is this why earth rescue circles can help them more easily than higher spirits? It seems rather dreadful.

That is true, but it is natural and governed by law. Think of air, water and earth which are separated states and, in a general way, one cannot penetrate the other. It is a natural law as with the various states of spirit. Higher spirits may with difficulty sometimes clothe themselves in a heavy garment more pertaining to matter and so penetrate the lower realms of spirit, but it is easier for them to work through earth people who are better attuned to those lower realms by their very nature being more material.

How can these souls best be helped then?

Help them now, in life. Let them be made aware of the truth. But if you meet them as spirits in your circles, tell them they have no material body now, but there is a heaven above them, a place of light to which they can go. Say to them, "Look up, look up to that light!" Then pray to the Shining Ones to come to their help and they will be led away.

CHAPTER TEN

Spiritual Understanding

So often we become discouraged in our efforts to go forward upon the spiritual pathway; there seem so many obstacles.

Some of you tread this way with a concentrated dedication while some walk the way with but a faint idea where they are going. Some see the glory of the revelation with a clear spirit vision; some behold it clothed only in the vision seen by others and which they desire to see too. Whatever may be the purpose with which you travel, remember that it is the travelling forward which is important, the effort put forth in the climb will eventually result in your upward journey.

The traveller upon the mountainside must sometimes pause and rest, waiting until some mighty power removes the obstacle in his pathway before he can go forward, and even so is it for those upon the spiritual way. You may have the clear sense of vision, the wish continually to climb, yet is there the insuperable barrier of personal responsibility which continually hems the soul in from exploration of the avenues of knowledge. We would say to remember that the obstacle upon the way, if bravely faced and patiently waited upon, will eventually be overcome, for there are mighty powers at work within the earthly life. Sometimes in the removal of some obstacle created by family conditions, it is the running rivulet of sorrow which removes the one who has held back the soul from its endeavour. Then must the soul hold fast and cling firmly unto its faith else it, too, will be torn away from the position it has attained, and swept down into the dark valleys of hopelessness and despair.

Hold fast to the knowledge that all things are working for good, although they appear sometimes to be working for evil, for the one who is truly dedicated, who has set his feet upon the climb to the top of the mountain, the pathway of spiritual truth, this one places himself or herself into touch with powers and forces as yet unknown to the mortal mind, but which are known to those who guide you forward.

When a time of great difficulty or trial emerges you are not alone, for around the aspiring soul converges a mighty host of strong spirits who have passed through just such an experience, and who stand by to strengthen and encourage, that the soul be not cast down. All things work together for good even in times of desolation and loss; what is important is that each one retains the desire to go forward and does not faint nor give up in this climb. The search for truth and illumination.

You speak of seeing a spiritual vision. I do not know quite what you mean.

Each soul has its own wish of attainment, a vision that hovers always before the spiritual eye. Unto some it is the reality of the being of the Master Jesus or the ability to compare their life to his. To others it is the realisation that their spirit has freed itself from the fetters of ancient thought and in this new revelation of truth and purity they may live, and sow into the earthly world the seed of love and kindliness, ceasing to reap the harvest of bitterness. To some it is simply the desire to live quietly and lovingly, no longer tempted by temptations of the smaller self, while to others comes the desire to press onward and upward unto a purer and closer realisation of their identity with the pure spirit, the Master Creator.

Whatever your wish, whatever your vision, go forward and know that in the inwardness of its meaning it is the love of the Great Creative Spirit calling home His children, drawing the soul nearer and nearer, back to its original unity in peace and power.

Are there any special virtues we should all try to cultivate?

You should each value and bless that particular quality of the soul individual unto yourself. So much earthly time is wasted in fruitlessly endeavouring to accomplish deeds done by others, or in trying to emulate writings of other men and women. When you feel you are of no value because of this, disappointment and despondency darken the inner soul.

Grains of sand are not meant to shine like stars in the firmament, nor daisies to give forth the perfume of a lily, nor yet the lily to twine like a climbing plant beautifying the branches of a tree. Each of you has a soul quality individual unto yourself, and it is this that needs to be understood and developed, that at last it may crystalise in the power of the spirit, becoming your shining jewel of experience, your treasure laid up in heaven.

Therefore, if the quality of your soul is simplicity: bless it. Let it stream forth in appreciation of the simple things of life, like a mountain river or a brook meandering through the woodside, refreshing and cleansing all it touches, thus revealing much that would otherwise be hidden. Eventually it can become the quality of revelation, often of mediumship, bringing forth crystal droplets of truth; and at the end of life's journey, on entering the spirit life, you may wear the diamond-like crystal symbolising the inner simplicity of your soul.

If gentleness is your soul quality, breathe it forth; do not hide it from the harshness of the world but speak gently, move quietly, and realise that gentleness has also the quality of peace, for are they not part of each other? In time love and healing develop, for many need the gentleness of an understanding heart to heal their inner soul. The tender pink and silver jewels will be the treasure of such a life.

Those who love know this is right, but not always do they understand how to bless this as it streams from them, for sometimes instead of a gentle warmth beautifying all whom they meet, their love is as a fire which burns and destroys. But still it should be treasured, for fire purifies and transmutes the baser elements, and those who have this fire within the soul develop healership, or love of humanity. Out of love is born the desire to serve and sacrifice, and from sacrifice comes the ruby jewel which will be their treasure in spirit. Truly, those who love may also be gentle, and the gentle may love truly, but you each have a predominant quality individual to yourself, and this needs to be appreciated and developed, that you may be yourself.

Some have strength, a deeply hidden perseverence which can be changed into endurance. Those who are strong often have to learn to stand firm, to consider, to think, to be still just where they are. Out of their stillness they develop discernment, not that of mediumship, but the deep inward discernment of the soul by which they see why great world changes occur, and changes within relationships of the earthly life. For them on the inner planes of spirit are formed the green jewels of patience and endurance, glowing like emeralds or jade.

The quality of peace is like an aureole of pure light. If this is the treasure of your being bless it, for tranquillity will flow around you in living streams of healing, eventually crystalising into the blue jewels of the soul. Often those who are innately peaceful feel they should seek for greater activity as they see their brothers and sisters running to and fro, and they are afraid to treasure their own inward quality, but peace is the basis of all healing.

To a few upon earth is given the quality of creativeness, of energy, but in their misunderstanding they seek for ever to be making something new, to be showing forth something different. Creativeness is the ability of the inner soul to become attuned unto the great rhythms continually flowing through the universe. The creative soul is like a listener, listening to the winds, to the waters, to the soul of the world, and then outspeaking that which they discern in streams of living music and poetry, in outpictured forms. But such souls become restless, sometimes destructive within themselves, because they do not fully understand how to bless the creativeness which moves in them. They should become attuned to the great rhythms, to the ebb and flow of eternal powers, that they may catch the golden stream of inspiration, turning it into the qualities of joy and appreciation, blending it with the other colours of the soul that all may gleam with golden light.

It may seem unto you that some of these creators, the musicians, and artists in your world, destroy themselves. This is because they know not how to hold in reverent love the very quality which makes them individual unto themselves.

Other qualities there are, but these of which I speak develop into the spiritual attributes known unto you, those which blossom into the beauties of mediumship, service, self-sacrifice and healership. Therefore, *be yourselves,* develop in the very fullness of your power, realising that from it other qualities may indeed begin to develop even as the petals of a flower unfold one by one, surrounding the inward heart of the blossom.

Many of those around me seem to lead full and useful lives, dedicated to the service of others. I feel inadequate and fail so often. What can I do? It is hard not to get depressed.

Unto all who feel within themselves inadequacy, weakness and failure I would say: These feelings, are they not all one and the same thing? For from them later will be born understanding, and out of understanding comes compassion, and from compassion is born love, and so you receive compensation even for your sense of weakness. Because you know this sense of inadequacy you will not despise your brothers and sisters when they seem to be weak, but rather from your own understanding you will say, "Yes, I know how you feel." So a bridge is made by which the green of sympathy, the rose pink of love and the tender hues of your healing flow from you to those others whom you meet.

In your secret moments of prayer say unto your Lord: Thanks for this failure, for this inadequacy, for I realise that from this I gain something by which I may help the progress of others upon the way.

I cannot understand what is meant by karma?

Within the law of karma, or sowing and reaping, there is to be found a deeper understanding of all the laws which govern your life, both spiritual and mortal.

The forgiveness of the human heart is small. It harbours within itself the sleeping memory of many hurts and wrongs, many injustices remembered in bitterness and pain, for the heart often forgets that the spirit of love is a spirit of forgiveness and it seeks to revenge itself for the hurts and wrongs which have been inflicted.

There is little forgiveness within the heart until it has been able to receive the great inflood of divine spiritual love which comes with the unfoldment of spiritual purpose and understanding. The essence of love is in the forgiveness of love, and the greater the lovingness the less can it perceive the small imperfections or hurts which come from contact with the mortal world.

Consider at the closing of the day: "How much has there been within the journey of this day which has brought unto me bitterness or hurt? Accordingly must be the stream of my forgiveness before I can remain in harmony with the Laws Divine." Also, as you come to the morning hours on the following day, consider: "This one who has hurt me. Shall I not now give unto that one some token of my forgiveness?"

Thus the spirit, progressing through the daily life, forges for itself a constant chain of loving forgiveness, the experiences falling behind the progress of the spirit in links of ever-changing light, touched here with the experience of the earth hurtful and bitter, and yet before the ending of the day changed again into the light of spiritual understanding by the pure touch of loving forgiveness.

The spirit who retaliates bitterness with bitterness sows into the ethers of life more pain and hurtfulness which will eventually come back again in further difficult experiences through which it must pass. Those who sow in love reap in love, and those who sow in forgiveness reap in forgiveness, for this is the law of the spirit.

How may we create a good future karma?

In the years before you come to self-realisation, you are inheritors of conditions created by those preceding you, and of conditions resulting from your past actions. But when you pause and say, "Who am I? Am I just a leaf blown in the winds of destiny or am I a spirit?" Then you begin to reverse the process of inheritance. Though you may continue to work through the past, now you begin to create those conditions that will be yours in the future.

So teach your people and your children that they must sow seeds of goodness, creative thought, kindness and lovingness, even though they are working through a difficult destiny in which they may be reaping a harvest of bitterness inherited from some previous time.

Perchance in your own home life there is chaos and unrest and you say, "How may the peace of spirit come into our lives?" First, you must learn to bless the very chaos surrounding you, looking at it with the clear perception of spiritual truth, seeing it not as particular injustice to yourself but as part of the whole unrest of your world. It will pass, for nothing in the earthly existence endures for ever, so bless the chaos and the very condition you resist. Set upon it your own wish for peace, and you will bring the light of spirit into the very condition from which you desire to escape.

After blessing with your mind, make a gesture with your hand, either touching the quarrelsome one or setting within the place of disharmony a visible symbol of your harmonious thought such as a little bunch of blossoms or a growing plant.

If you desire to create prosperity in the years to come, give thanks for what you have and for hands with which you can labour. Then make some token of your gratitude by labouring a little more for those who need care, perhaps cooking a little extra for those poorer than yourself. Bless your labour, but give away part of what you produce. Do not think, "I can only attain a small amount of money, therefore I must keep it for the future," but bless part of it and give it lovingly to others with greater need. Thus as you live and move into the future you may inherit the result of this that you are creating in the present.

Again, some of you fear the loneliness of old age, but using the wisdom of understanding you must learn to bless the relationships that are with you now. Sometimes in your heart you cry: "These relationships of family and responsibility. These do not bring me joy. This is not what I want." But you should bless those who try your patience, who bring you tears of disappointment, for this develops within your soul the capacity to endure and to understand. Give thanks on your knees for those who bring you joy, and for those whose hearts melt in the tenderness of love in unity with you own.

As you bless and give thanks to the great Master Spirit, so are you setting into motion the great flowing vibrations that go out into the future, and as you move onward you will meet others who need your understanding and understand them by reason of the difficulties you have endured.

Do not limit yourselves to those who now hold your hands, the beloveds of your heart: you must be prepared to bless them, let them go, move on, for in the future the great Giver of All Good will bring you friends, companionship, and the conditions that you yourself may desire. Always by your right acceptance and lack of resentment as to the present, you set into motion the great powers of creative vibration which go on and on into the future. As you move through time so you come to meet that which is good, sweet and noble.

Sow with the seed of nobility: let your earth be glad that you dwell for a little while, imparting unto the living soil some part of your own touch of blessing.

Is it good to love even if that love is not reciprocated?

The outpouring of love is far more important than its receiving, for the spiritual law of love is to give and go on giving, for what is given circles round in a mighty circle of light and eventually returns unto the one from whom it sprung. Unto all who love and gain no return for their loving, I would say: Keep on loving! Send it out and it will flow in a great circle of radiant light and some day it will return again to you, for nothing can be given but what eventually it must find its point of return. Round and round upon the great spirals of human progression, upon the great spirals of creative energy, round and round go the starry forms of light and the great loves of men and women, always meeting on higher vibrations, lifting, transmuting, changing all things, but always working according to the pattern and law of the great Creator.

Life seems to hold such long stretches of drabness when nothing important happens.

It is not that which happens to you which is of importance, it is your reaction unto that circumstance. See always that your reaction conforms to the law of love, and give for unkindness, kindness; give for cruelty, forgiveness; give for darkness, light, and remember that the law of love is the law of giving rather than receiving.

As you give forth your love in a richness of blessing, an outpouring of gifts, in healing and encouragement, you will find that the true joy of your life is in the deep inward satisfaction which is gained in giving the best you have unto those in need, and unto those who can receive. For in this giving forth in joy you live according to the true identity of your inward soul.

Sometimes it seems however much effort we put into working for what seems right, there is so little to show for it.

You will never see in your earthly world the results of your labours, for that which is done with spiritual intent is done unto the spirit, and may not be fruited upon earth. The man who builds for himself great wealth upon earth will reap the wealth of the earth, but the one who gives his labour in love and service unto others, to men and women who pass swiftly from his comprehension, such a one will only see the result of his sowing in the spiritual realm when the journey of earth is over. It should be that you in your wisdom will be content to labour, to love and to sow within the field of human life the seed of goodness, that your reaping may come by and by, for on the earth there is only the shadow, whilst here within the spirit is the reality. Therefore your work must ever be incomplete. The wise spirit says: "I live here within a world in which all is change, for that is the law of the Master Spirit. So I will not grieve either over gain or loss, either over riches nor yet over poverty, but rather will I seek in all things to accomplish with a loving spirit the labours which come unto my hand."

Why is the earthly life so fraught with difficulty and frustration?

Many of you who are learning your lessons in the great school of life question this. Your world needs to manifest the spiritual aspects of love, and the first of these is patience. In order to help you lift your love on to a higher plane, the things you desire are withheld for a time that you may learn to wait in patience and in peace, for truly in patience there *is* peace.

Often the ways of the earthly life show forth this lesson, when the lover is separated from the beloved through war, economic stress, or the differences of race. By this separation the beloved learns patiently to wait. When a beloved precedes you into the life of spirit through disease or accident, because you know the spirit endures for ever, you wait patiently for months and years, quietly persisting in the knowledge that you will meet again with the coming of your own death.

So love teaches you patience and patience teaches you peace. In your development of the spiritual powers of healing and mediumship you need to learn their higher manifestations, but always you cry aloud saying, "Why does it take so long before the healing brings health and ease to the ones we desire to help?" It would be wiser to ask yourself: "Have I sufficient love for these sufferers to keep on healing in patience and peace? Is my love really for myself, in that I desire to see the result of my healing rebounding unto my own benefit and praise?"

To our vision patience fills the aura with a shade of gentle green, a colour to be seen in the world of nature where there is no hurry, no haste, for the grass comes slowly to fruition and the leaf unfolds in unresisting silence. This is the greenness of beauty in your world, and even so is it seen within the spiritual aura. When it slowly changes to these delicate green hues, we see expansion and strength coming there and we blend into that aura any other colour, for there is no clash between another colour and green, for this is the beauty of its being. We sometimes blend in the deeper blues to stimulate psychic unfoldment, rose pink to warm and quicken the affections, the gold of wisdom and the deep mauve shades of healing. Therefore one of your first lessons before you may become a medium or healer is this lesson of patience.

Whatever your condition of earthly life, bless your time of trial or of waiting, thank the Master Creator for witholding the treasures which you desire, for in the waiting you may learn patience, and in learning patience you will find peace.

Is there a golden rule for living?

Try to order your lives as harmlessly as possible. Learn to have a quiet tongue which if it cannot speak good will remain silent. Learn to have such love within your heart that it can quench the raging fire of your temper and resentfulness, that unto the unjust accusations of others and in the quarrelsome situations that arise you may stem the fire of your impatience, the swiftness of your retort, for those who live harmlessly will not engage in quarrels with other men and women. Truly you may give wisdom and quietness of judgement, but not in the heat of debate or the haste of impatience.

Blessed is the peacemaker, but how may he be blessed unless he has such peace within his heart that he sees no reason to quarrel? In living harmlessly, sometimes in the secrecy of prayer you must decide between two situations, and it may seem whichever decision you make this will bring hurt unto another human soul. To apply the laws of love and peace your decision will be made so that the least harm and hurt may be rendered unto all whom you know. Then having made your decision in the tenderness of love and prayer, extend unto the one you need to hurt the healing of your love, the gentleness of your regret. Thus you bring the law of harmlessness into the fullness of its fruition and beauty.

If one learns to guard the tongue and say nothing harmful, isn't the damage already done if the thought has been there?

This is partly true, but I think it is impossible for earth's children in their present state of development to make every thought harmless. It is easier to begin with the heart and deed, then with the word, then as you grow in strength and power slowly the harmlessness may be transferred into the more subtle regions of the soul self, and may come forth in thought, prayer and love. But it is always good to try to feel, speak and think harmlessly.

If one does say something that is regretted, is it possible to lessen its effect by sending out the counteracting thought?

Yes, each of you should try to live in such a way that at the closure of each day, if anything has been done or said which you recognise as harmful, try to cancel and change it. Either ask the person harmed for their forgiveness, or change the wrong thought by a thought of love and healing, for by so doing you balance the scales of cause and effect day by day, bringing the mind and soul back into harmony.

Can perfect health be gained by the power of thought?

No, not by the power of thought, but it can be gained by the purification of thought so that the thought body comes into harmony with the spirit which is trying to express itself through the thought and emotional bodies.

One simple way to attain this harmony is to cultivate the habit of non-action. Refrain as much as possible from giving forth any reaction into the outer world until you have paused to analyse that which has taken place. When in your passage along a street, although the pavement is nearly empty, another walks straight into you, your first reaction will be to say to yourself, "This man is not looking where he is going, therefore I have the right to be annoyed with him." But if you follow the policy of non-action, then you will stop and think, "Was he drawn to me by a ray of attraction, and have I then a service to render unto him?" This would be a policy of non-action by you to give your spirit time to consider that which had occurred. So also in all similar incidents of the day; the spirit, as onlooker, viewing the whole picture of life, stands and considers each happening before any reaction occurs within the mind or feeling.

Thus your spirit may fully judge what has occurred before it allows a reaction to take place, and in such a fashion your reaction must always be of a spiritual nature.

Is suffering necessary?

It is true that you must pass through varying experiences in the daily life but you do not need to suffer; your suffering is simply your reaction to what occurs. Throughout your whole life there will be changes of pattern, for your children will grow up and leave you; your mother and father will one day be transferred into spirit. Sometimes other men and women will not understand you and you will react either with sorrow or bitterness to these things. But if you are wise you will say to yourself, "These are but experiences which come to every person; they come to develop strength within me." By accepting them you do not need to suffer. You just endure them as a means by which your soul will be more highly developed.

I have heard it said that suffering is ordained by God.

God has not ordained suffering, but has ordained change, change which must come in every human life. But there is no need for you to suffer through these changes if you can accept them as experiences by which you learn.

Surely suffering helps one to have compassion for another who suffers similarly?

To answer this question we must understand what we mean by suffering, for surely the inner meaning is to endure agonising pain of mind or body, and I would say this is *not* necessary. People suffer because they try to withstand conditions arising in their life, but if they can accept these things as something through which they will learn, they may know pain and loneliness, they may endure separation, but they need not suffer in the full meaning of the word. Therefore, the soul by passing through varying experiences enlarges its understanding and gains in tolerance of others, but it endures suffering only because it will not accept.

As we pass middle age, many of us find our memory failing. It is very worrying. Will it hinder our spiritual development?

This should not cause anxiety for it is part of the spiritual growth of the soul that it may learn how to forget as well as how to remember. Often we have to take souls who have newly arrived in the spirit life and deliberately teach them to forget. In the Halls of Forgetfulness where a soft, silvery grey light fills the atmosphere, those who need to have unpleasant memories eradicated from their minds rest for awhile in dim hospital rooms where slowly the consciousness sinks into rest, rest, deeper and deeper rest, until at last it begins to let go of its earth memories of pain and fear. When this period is completed, skilled healers will draw from the sleeping mind the residue of the memory. If such a one returns to earth to communicate, you may discover it does not remember dying or the seasons of pain, but comes back with remembrance of happy and joyful things. This lesson of forgetfulness is of great importance.

As you make your way through the many experiences of the daily life seeking spiritual unfoldment, the habit of remembering spiritual matters becomes established, but with it you may forget certain earthly things which no longer seem of trememdous importance to the spiritual mind. If you understood this with greater wisdom you would command yourself to remember or forget, saying: "This is of no value. I will let it go and forget it." Thus the consciousness would be uncluttered and free to remember that which is important.

In your schools the child and youth should be taught the value of forgetfulness. Too often when souls come newly to the spirit life they are tormented by remembrance of unimportant details of their mortal life. We say to them: "Forget it. Think upon the things of the spirit. Look to the glorious light and remember the new truths we are trying to teach you." But because the old habit of thought is so strong it will continue until it is at last transmuted.

As your pass from youth to maturity and thence to the closing years, try to apply this truth to your lives with wisdom, cultivating the memory of your spiritual consciousness, learning to forget the less important mortal things. Furthermore, this habit of not forgetting can create mental torment for those still in the physical body.

When you desire to help just such a sleepless sufferer, send unto them the soft, silvery grey colours of rest, deep rest, and impart into the consciousness by thought the idea, "Forget your suffering, let go of your fear." Draw it unto your self as a healer, even as the healers in spirit draw from the consciousness of the resting soul its memory. You can also withdraw from a sick person the remembered fear or pain they endured in a difficult illness or operation, and so hasten their recovery. The veil of forgetfulness can be drawn across the mind like a soft, silvery grey blanket, as you draw away from them the memory of their suffering.

You who desire to heal often think, "Oh, could we but take away the memory of guilt, sorrow and suffering, and replace it with harmony and happiness." You can indeed, but first apply this simple law unto yourselves, that in the valuation of forgetting and remembering will come the seed of your wisdom.

Why can we not remember our past lives, the experiences we had before we were born?

Surely the burden of remembrance is very great! Would it be wise to be burdened by remembering all the errors and mistakes, the triumphs, joys and sorrows of the life preceding this one? The Master Creator in His love taught man to draw the veil of forgetfulness that he may take his way on earth with a fresh and new consciousness, one able to absorb experiences, then to forget them, that newer and better ones may be absorbed. Give thanks to the great Giver of all Good that He has given you the power to forget as well as to remember.

The consciousness of man is like a tree, which, if it is to grow straight and strong and glorious must shed some part of itself ere ever it may unfold the higher and newer parts. Man's new consciousness unfolds from the old one of things he has forgotten. Forgetfulness is the soil from which grows the plant of wisdom, realisation and new remembering.

There are many teachings on the value of peace and joy, but what about laughter? Isn't this of spiritual value?

The birthright of those seeking understanding of spiritual law should be the way of quiet happiness and joyful peace. But man's mind becomes contained within the shell of its own sorrow and self-concern. For this reason the Master Spirit sends to the earth those whom you know as the laughter makers, the clowns, those having deep within themselves the ability to create joy and laughter wherever they go. When laughter moves within the inward being and a host of people enter into joy and amusement together, then the joy within reaches unto the joy without. This creates an opening, an opportunity, whereby the mightier spiritual joy may find entrance. Value your laughter makers, for they are part of the great healing band which encircles your sorrowful world.

Have they any special work to do in the spirit world?

When they leave the mortal body and continue their life in the spirit places they go on creating laughter and bringing to birth happiness. Sometimes they come to your circles, awakening the laughter which may bring true inward relaxation and release from tensions. But they do their greatest work here within the astral planes and within the homes of healing in the first planes of spirit experience, for to these places come those who leave the mortal body shattered by sorrow or broken in mind by lack of understanding, or with the memory of great suffering. We cannot gain their attention to teach them the laws of spirit, but unto such we bring the laughter makers, those who can create such fun, such an exaggeration of joy that those watching must eventually give way to a little amusement, and finally unto a little laughter. So the creator of laughter who was once a comedian of the earth can give the sad one some part of their own golden joy. This will be the start of the rehabilitation of the soul stricken in sorrow.

Do we weaken others by helping them?

The true way to help one another is in standing by and giving hope when it seems that all is hopeless, in upholding them when they are cast down into the depths of weakness and despair, by lending unto them strength, so that they have the power to continue from day to day until the time of trial is past.

To feed the hungry over an idefinite period of time is to supply their need but to deprive them of the desire and necessity to work. Work and labour should be undertaken with love, for that is the expression of the inward spiritual will through which the great laws of cause and effect are continually balanced. Where there is no need to labour, then lethargy and self-indulgence seize upon the mind, body and soul, and with that comes destructiveness and sinfulness.

We in the spirit love you, but our labour of love is rendered not by removing your responsibilities but by standing by and lending unto you hope, strength and comfort, by shedding light upon you and interpenetrating your world with radiations of peace. We know that through such spiritual influence slowly you become stronger and able to stand in your own right as beautiful spirits, and out of your own experience of suffering will develop the desire and ability to comfort others. So do not *seek* to try to help one another. Be wise in your helping, and know that if in your desire and ability to assist you yourself are being dragged down and exhausted, then you do not serve in wisdom, because you are not helping the other ones to understand and help themselves.

Regarding our attitude to possessions, we know there should be non-attachment, but is it not equally important to cultivate this toward people?

Truly, for sometimes in the treasures of the heart there must come a willingness to relinquish one who is well-beloved and who is, perhaps, of greater value to the soul than all their possessions or gifts.

How can we recognise the right time for this?

It is an attitude of the inward consciousness, a willingness to relinquish if this should be demanded. It is an inward feeling that although this beloved one is indeed the treasure of the heart, yet does he or she rightly belong unto the Master Creator. Should it be that this one is demanded, then there must be the willingness to let go. It is not always necessary that the relinquishment should take place, but rather the attitude within the spiritual self which is important.

Let your thought go forth in healing unto other creatures of the earth and let your living magnetic force radiate unto all things that you see and all things that you touch. Do not live unto yourselves alone, but live as part of the whole, and as part of the whole let goodness, love and peace be your watchword.

How would you answer the question "Am I my brother's keeper?"

It is good and it is right that each of you who are upon the pathway of unfoldment should learn to become a guardian or keeper of their brother, a leader of the wandering sheep. Consider with what care the shepherd looks after his sheep, planning the pastures wherein they may feed, and yet are the sheep all unheeding of his tending, aware of him only when confusion seizes upon them and the flock becomes scattered. Then are they glad to hear the familiar voice calling them home, bringing them once more into unity with each other and with him.

Even so are you here in the mortal life, for you are the shepherds of the sheep and yet the sheep are unaware of your shepherding. The law of love is expressed by unity, and you cannot live unto yourself alone for this will bring spiritual stagnation. If you have loved, if you are upon the spiritual pathway, you can only progress by becoming the guardian, the leader, teacher or keeper of the flock of your heedless brothers and sisters around you. But if you have not yet evolved love within your heart, if you are still living the ordinary life of the animal creature, then you are *not* a keeper of the flock for you are but a goat or a sheep yourself who has to be lovingly led forward and brought into the pathways of understanding. Those who have not yet learned the law of love, these too become their brother's keepers and sad and sorrowful is the pattern they portray, keeping their brother in the chains of their possessiveness and selfishness.

So, you are the keeper of your brother's destiny whilst you are growing in love and unity, and also whilst you are showing the opposite aspect of love which is love jealous, love possessive, the love which holds and clings. Whichever way humanity treads it still has this responsibility, for no human soul can progress along the pathway unless they bring another with them. Nothing occurs without each man and woman contributing something to the total joy or misery; each is responsible for the whole pattern outworked within the town, village or place they call their own.

That is a hard teaching. Is it not contrary to the law of personal responsibility?

No, that is not true. In this sea of mortal experience you cannot live unto yourself alone. You are part of the great community of life surrounding you, interpenetrating your thought, touching your aura, flowing through your physical body. As you progress, your understanding of the law of personal responsibility will come more and more into an attunement with the great Giver of all Good, until your purified love becomes a universal compassion for the people around you. As this flows from you into the great sea of human life, you betray your knowledge that you are the keeper of the flocks, the shepherd of the sheep, for you are the keeper of the brother and sister nearest to you, shepherding them on the way towards the light. They may be unaware of your influence even as the sheep who follow close behind the shepherd as he quietly goes forward. You may say you do not possess them and they do not belong to you; nevertheless, in your spiritual influence you show that you are your brother's keeper, keeping him in the way of truth and beauty.

What about the guiding ones in spirit? Are you your brother's keeper?

Yes, yes! We are the keepers of those in the mortal life, for we know that before we can come into a closer kinship with the great Spirit of Joy we must firstly bring home from their wandering way some of the weak, the lost and the hungry, by interpenetrating our silent influence into their consciousness that the good therein may be stimulated to unfold and grow strong, and that they may see the way and walk the paths which lead to the things of the spirit.

A Group Prayer

"We would gather together the scattered petals of thought created by the consciousness of all who are here, bringing them together in one beautiful blossom that they may be joined into the stem of our teaching, thus creating a lovely flower enfolded in the soft green leaves of sympathy that wing from the hearts and thoughts of those present. As we create this beautiful blossom, like a lovely chrysanthemum glowing with the purity of light and tinged with the gentle pink of love, we would uplift it, O thou Great Creator, that this bloom may be taken unto the altars of prayer in the temple of light, there to lie for a time gleaming and glistening with the blessing which comes from Thee."

Other teachings by spirit Ramadahn:

Spiritual Virtues in the Aura. These collected lectures explain the way in which people develop spiritual qualities amid the experiences of daily life, and the manner in which the aura reveals soul qualities such as courage, perseverance, tolerance and generosity. A small but very valuable book.

Colour and healing in the New Age: Trance lectures by Ramadahn describing colour emanations emanating from Spirit, and the way they may affect the individual human aura.

Also Single lecture transcripts: all available from the Atlantis Bookshop. 49A Museum Street, London WC1A 2SE.